Ready-to-Use

VOCABULARY, WORD ATTACK & COMPREHENSION ACTIVITIES

Sixth Grade Reading Level

HENRIETTE L. ALLEN, Ph. D.
WALTER B. BARBE, Ph. D.
M. THERESE A. LEVESQUE, Ph. D.

THE CENTER FOR APPLIED RESEARCH IN EDUCATION
West Nyack, New York 10994

Library of Congress Cataloging-in-Publication Data

Allen, Henriette L.
   Ready-to-use vocabulary, word analysis & comprehension activities
/ Henriette L. Allen, Walter B. Barbe, Linda Lehner.
      p.   cm. — (Reading skills activities library)
   Contents: [1] First grade reading level — [2] Second grade
reading level — [3] Third grade reading level.
   ISBN 0-87628-932-4 (v. 1). — ISBN 0-87628-933-2 (v. 2). — ISBN
0-87628-934-0 (v. 3)
   1. Reading (Elementary)—Problems, exercises, etc.   2. Reading
comprehension—Problems, exercises, etc.   3. Vocabulary—Study and
teaching (Elementary)—Problems, exercises, etc.   I. Barbe, Walter
Burke, 1926–   .   II. Lehner, Linda.   III. Title.   IV. Series.
LB1573.A44   1996
372.4—dc20   96-18332
                                                       CIP

© 1998 *by* The Center for Applied Research in Education, West Nyack, NY

Printed in the United States of America

10 9 8 7 6 5 4 3 2 1

ISBN 0-87628-479-9

ATTENTION: CORPORATIONS AND SCHOOLS

The Center for Applied Research in Education books are available at quantity discounts with bulk
purchase for educational, business, or sales promotional use. For information, please write to:
Prentice Hall Special Sales, 240 Frisch Court, Paramus, NJ 07652. Please supply: title of book,
ISBN number, quantity, how the book will be used, date needed.

**THE CENTER FOR APPLIED RESEARCH
IN EDUCATION**
West Nyack, NY 10994
A Simon & Schuster Company

On the World Wide Web at http://www.phdirect.com

Prentice Hall International (UK) Limited, *London*
Prentice Hall of Australia Pty. Limited, *Sydney*
Prentice Hall Canada, Inc., *Toronto*
Prentice Hall Hispanoamericana, S.A., *Mexico*
Prentice Hall of India Private Limited, *New Delhi*
Prentice Hall of Japan, Inc., *Tokyo*
Simon & Schuster Asia Pte. Ltd., *Singapore*
Editora Prentice Hall do Brasil, Ltda., *Rio de Janeiro*

About the
READING SKILLS
ACTIVITIES LIBRARY

The "Reading Skills Activities Library" is designed to give classroom teachers, reading specialists, and others who teach reading multiple learning activities to build specific reading skills at each grade level, first through sixth grade. Each grade level unit provides 200 or more reproducible reading and writing activities to help children master reading skills that can be used with *any* reading program.

FIRST LEVEL   ***Ready-to-Use Vocabulary, Word Analysis & Comprehension Activities*—FIRST GRADE READING LEVEL**

SECOND LEVEL ***Ready-to-Use Vocabulary, Word Analysis & Comprehension Activities*—SECOND GRADE READING LEVEL**

THIRD LEVEL   ***Ready-to-Use Vocabulary, Word Analysis & Comprehension Activities*—THIRD GRADE READING LEVEL**

FOURTH LEVEL ***Ready-to-Use Vocabulary, Word Attack & Comprehension Activities*—FOURTH GRADE READING LEVEL**

FIFTH LEVEL   ***Ready-to-Use Vocabulary, Word Attack & Comprehension Activities*—FIFTH GRADE READING LEVEL**

SIXTH LEVEL   ***Ready-to-Use Vocabulary, Word Attack & Comprehension Activities*—SIXTH GRADE READING LEVEL**

The skill activities follow the sequence in the Barbe Reading Skills Check List developed by nationally known educator Walter B. Barbe, Ph.D. The activities can be assigned to individuals or groups and supervised by the teacher, a paraprofessional, a parent, a volunteer, or a peer.

Each grade level unit of Reading Skills Activities includes:

1. Directions for using the reading activities at that level to support direct instruction
2. At least 200 reproducible activities for quick, reliable practice or enrichment of each reading skill, with answer keys at the end
3. A reproducible Barbe Reading Skills Check List for the major skill areas covered at that level for easy individual or group recordkeeping

You will find that the "Reading Skills Activities Library" provides for:

- Quick, accurate prescriptive help to meet specific reading needs
- A minimum of four ready-to-use reading skills exercises to reinforce, supplement, and enrich instruction in each skill
- Flexibility in planning individual and group activities, homework assignments, and peer- or aide-assisted instruction

The activities can be used by the teacher, parent or reading specialist in any learning setting, in any manner the teacher deems most appropriate. The activities are meant to provide handy, efficient, systematic help in developing reading skills that students need to become proficient readers.

Henriette L. Allen
Walter B. Barbe

About the Authors

Henriette L. Allen, Ph.D., is a former classroom teacher in the schools of Coventry, Rhode Island, the Aramco Schools of Dhahran, Saudi Arabia, The American Community School of Benghazi, Libya, and Jackson, Mississippi.

Dr. Allen served in several administrative roles, including assistant superintendent of the Jackson Public Schools. She is presently an education consultant recognized nationally. Dr. Allen is the senior author of the series *Competency Tests for Basic Reading Skills* (West Nyack, NY: The Center for Applied Research in Education.) She has taught reading skills at both elementary and secondary levels, has supervised the development of a Continuous Progress Reading Program for the Jackson Public Schools, and has lectured widely in the fields of reading, classroom management, technology in the classroom, and leadership in educational administration. Dr. Allen is listed in the *World Who's Who of Women* and *Who's Who—School District Officials*. She was the 1996 recipient of the Distinguished Service Award given by the American Association of School Administrators.

A nationally known authority in the fields of reading and learning disabilities, **Walter B. Barbe, Ph.D.,** was for twenty-five years editor-in-chief of the widely acclaimed magazine *Highlights for Children* and adjunct professor at The Ohio State University. Dr. Barbe is the author of over 150 professional articles and a number of books, including *Personalized Reading Instruction* (West Nyack, NY: Parker Publishing Company, Inc.), coauthored with Jerry L. Abbot. He is also the senior author and editor of two series—*Creative Growth with Handwriting* (Columbus, OH: Zaner-Bloser, Inc.) and *Barbe Reading Skills Check Lists and Activities* (West Nyack, NY: The Center for Applied Research in Education)—and the senior editor of *Competency Tests for Basic Reading Skills*. Dr. Barbe is a fellow of the American Psychological Association and is listed in *Who's Who in America* and *American Men of Science*.

M. Therese A. Levesque, Ph.D., has had 25 years of experience as a language teacher and administrator in the schools of Coventry, Rhode Island, and the schools of Chenango Forks and South Orangetown, New York. She has successively held positions as Language Department Chairperson, Assistant Principal, Middle School Principal, Title III Director, and Assistant Superintendent. Her activities include preparation of New York State Regents Examinations, curriculum development, and directing programs focused on reading. She is listed in *Who's Who of American Women*.

Contents

Contents

How to Use These
Reading Skills Activities
Most Effectively

The learning activities in this unit can help you make optimal use of time in helping each of your students learn to read. The first requirement for a positive learning situation is, of course, your own enthusiastic teaching. Nothing replaces that. However, the student must apply what has been taught. Instruction must be followed through. Practice is needed in order to be sure that a skill has not only been learned but mastered.

In order for skills to develop sequentially, it is vital that you know where a student is within the sequence of reading skills. The Barbe Reading Skills Check List and practice activities in this unit provide a practical and systematic means to meet the specific reading skill needs of each of your pupils on a continuing, day-to-day basis.

The reading activities offer ready-to-use opportunities to learn, practice, and master the vocabulary, word attack, and comprehension skills at the sixth grade level, including at least four pages of practice work directed to each skill. Each activity is tailored to meet the learning needs of students at the sixth grade level. The activities provide complete, easy-to-follow student directions and may be duplicated as many times as needed for individual or group use. Complete answer keys are provided at the end of the unit.

The Barbe Reading Skills Check List is *not* intended as a rigid instructional program. Rather, it is meant to offer a general pattern around which a program may be built. The check list may be used to verify (1) where the student is in a sequence of reading skills, (2) when the student masters the skills, and (3) the number of skills mastered.

A copy of the Barbe Reading Skills Check List: SIXTH LEVEL is on pages 12–13 for your optional use.

IDENTIFYING INDIVIDUAL READING NEEDS

Before planning an instructional program for any pupil, it is necessary to determine at what level the student is reading. This may be accomplished through the use of an informal reading inventory. Many such informal assessment devices are provided in *Alternative Assessment Techniques for Reading & Writing* (West Nyack, NY: The Center for Applied Research in Education, 1996), by Wilma H. Miller.

Once a pupil's areas of difficulty are identified, instruction can then be planned, taught, and reinforced through practice. When the student has worked through a unit of instruction, a posttest to verify mastery of the skill may be given. When mastery occurs, the student progresses to another skill. When the student is unsuccessful in a specific reading skill and a reasonable amount of instruction does not result in mastery, it may be that a different instructional method or approach is needed, or a preliminary skill needs reevaluation followed by additional teaching-learning activities.

TEACHING AND REINFORCING SKILLS

After a reading skill has been identified as lacking, the teaching-learning process begins. The skill may be taught using the basal reader, selected children's literature, and/or your reading program as the basic source of information. Explaining the skill, giving the rules which apply, and illustrating by examples are frequently used techniques. The next step in the teaching-learning process is to assign an activity with which the student can try his or her wings at learning. The activity indicates if the learning has occurred or verifies that the student understands the lesson. When the student meets that particular situation in a reading selection, he or she can apply the appropriate reading skill.

At this point in the learning process, the reading skills activities should become a valuable teaching asset. They include several pages of practice exercises for every reading objective on the reading skills check list as well as those found in every reading program. You can select the exercises specifically designed to aid students at their particular level of reading development. After the paper-and-pencil activities are completed—during class time, as a homework assignment, as a cooperative learning activity, or as a peer instruction activity—results of the learning activity should be discussed with the student. You can then prescribe additional practice for the skill, reteach the skill, or proceed to the next activity.

RECORDKEEPING ON THE SKILLS CHECK LIST

Recordkeeping is an important part of any instructional design. Simplicity and ease are vital. One suggested method for marking the skills check list is as follows.

III. Comprehension:
    A. Outlining
        1. Takes notes effectively
        2. Can sequence ideas or events
        3. Can skim for specific purposes:
            a. To locate facts and details
            b. To select and reject materials to fit a certain purpose
        4. Can identify main ideas of paragraphs
        5. Can interpret characters' feelings
        6. Can identify topic sentences
    B. Following Directions

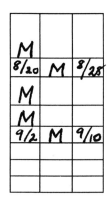

Put an *M* in the first column if the pupil takes a test and demonstrates mastery of that basic reading skill. If the pupil has not mastered the skill, record the date. The date in the first column then indicates when instruction in the skill began. When the pupil is tested a second time, put an *M* in the second column if mastery is achieved and record the date of mastery in the next column. Thus, anyone looking at the check list can tell whether the student mastered the skill before instruction or after instruction began, and when the skill was actually mastered.

Barbe Reading Skills Check List
SIXTH LEVEL

On the following pages you will find the Barbe Reading Skills Check List: SIXTH LEVEL. A group or individual recordkeeping form, "Class Record of Reading Skills: SIXTH LEVEL," is also provided on pages 291–301.

Together, these forms offer a practical and optional individual and group record-keeping system for pinpointing students' reading progress throughout the school year. They provide a useful guide to instruction as well as a basis for conferences with other faculty, parents, and the student about the pupil's reading progress. These records can also be passed along to the next grade level teacher at the end of the year to provide evidence of where students are in the continuum of reading skills.

BARBE READING SKILLS CHECK LIST
SIXTH LEVEL*

_____   _____   _____
(Last Name)   (First Name)   (Name of School)

_____   _____   _____
(Age)   (Grade Placement)   (Name of Teacher)

I. Vocabulary:

A. Word Recognition
  1. Uses context clues
    a. How the word is used in a sentence
    b. Function of the word
  2. Uses configuration clues
    a. Visual impressions of words
    b. Shape, length of words
  3. Uses language rhythms
    a. Rhyming clues
    b. Appreciation for general rhythm of well-expressed ideas

B. Knows and Uses Prefixes and Suffixes

Prefix	Meaning	Suffix	Meaning
ab	from, away	able, ible	capable of being
an	without, not	acy, ace, ancy, ance	state of being
ad	to, toward	an, ean, ian	one who
ante	before	age	act or condition
bi	two, twice	ant	n.—one who
circum	around	er, ar	relating to, like
de	from	ary	n.—one who—(place where)
dis	apart, not		adj.—relating to one who is little, made
dia	around	en	one who is little, made
ex	out of, from	ence	state of quality
im	not, in	ent	adj.—being, n.—one who
il, un, in, ir	into, not	ful	full of
inter	between	fy, ify	to make
in, en	in, into, among	hood	state, condition
intro	within, against	ic	like, made of
mis	wrong, wrongly	ice	that which, quality or state of being
non	not	id	being in a condition of
pan	whole, all	ion	act or state of being
per	fully, through	ize, ise	to make
peri	around, about	ist, ite	one who
post	after, behind	ity, ty	state
pre	before	ive	relating to
pro	for, in front of	less	without
re	back, again	ly	in a way
se	aside	ment	act or state of being
semi	half, partly	ness	state of being
sub	under	or, ar, er, ory	one who, that which
super	over, above	ose, ous	abounding in
trans	beyond, across	some	full of
tri	three, thrice	ward	turning to, in direction
un	not	y	like or full of

C. Word Meaning
  1. Knows multiple meanings of words
  2. Can associate words and feelings
  3. Formal and informal language
    a. Identifies different speech patterns
    b. Understands level of language usage
  4. Distinguishes between aided and unaided recall
  5. Can hyphenate words
  6. Can provide synonyms
  7. Can provide antonyms

       *© 1998 Walter B. Barbe, Honesdale, PA 18431

8. Understands homophones (same sound, different spelling: *some—sum*)
9. Understands homographs (same spelling, different meaning: run *fast—fast* from food)
10. Can write metaphors
11. Can write similes

II. Word Attack:
A. Phonic and Structural Characteristics of Words
  1. Knows initial consonants and blends
  2. Knows short and long vowels
B. Vowel Sounds
  1. Knows vowel rules
     a. When there is only one vowel in a word or syllable, the vowel is short
     b. When there are two vowels in a word or syllable, the first vowel is long and the second is silent
     c. When there are two vowels together, the first is long and the second is silent
C. Syllabication
  1. Knows rules for syllables
     a. Each syllable must have a vowel and a single vowel can be a syllable
     b. The root is a syllable and is not divided
     c. Blends are not divided (*th, str, wh*, etc.)
     d. Suffixes and prefixes are syllables
     e. Suffix *-ed* if preceded by a single *d* or *t* usually forms a separate syllable (*rest ed*)
     f. If a vowel in a syllable is followed by two consonants, the syllable ends with the first consonant
     g. If a vowel in a syllable is followed by only one consonant, the syllable ends with the vowel
     h. If a word ends in *le*, the consonant just before the *l* begins the last syllable (*ta-ble, han-dle*)
     i. When there is an *r* after a vowel, the *r* goes with the vowel
D. Knows Accent Rules
  1. In a word of two or more syllables, the first syllable is usually accented unless it is a prefix
  2. In most two-syllable words that end in a consonant followed by *y*, the first syllable is accented and the last is unaccented
  3. Beginning syllables *de, re, be, er, in* and *a* are usually not accented
  4. When a suffix is added, the accent falls on or within the root word
  5. Endings that form syllables are usually unaccented
  6. When a final syllable ends in *le*, that syllable is usually not accented
E. Knows Possessives
F. Knows Contractions
G. Knows Silent Letters
H. Knows Glossary

III. Comprehension:
A. Outlining
  1. Takes notes effectively
  2. Can sequence ideas or events
  3. Can skim for specific purposes
     a. To locate facts and details
     b. To select and reject materials to fit a certain purpose
  4. Can identify main ideas of paragraphs
  5. Can interpret characters' feelings
  6. Can identify topic sentences
B. Following Directions
C. Drawing Conclusions
D. Reading for Verification
E. Locating Information
  1. Reference material
     a. Can read and interpret graphs
     b. Can read and interpret maps
     c. Can locate materials in encyclopedia
     d. Uses dictionary regularly
  2. Library skills
     a. Uses card catalog
     b. Understands book classification system
  3. Periodical reading
     a. Reads newspapers regularly
     b. Knows major sections of newspapers
     c. Reads magazines regularly
     d. Uses periodicals for current information
F. Can Read Proof Marks

paragraph	upper-case
delete	lower-case
insert	transpose
insert period	insert comma

Vocabulary, Word Attack
& Comprehension
Activities
SIXTH LEVEL

The following activities will help you give students practice in the specific vocabulary, word attack, and comprehension skills at the SIXTH LEVEL. These materials provide for the following:

- Learning activities for specific reading skills
- Individual and group practice and/or enrichment
- Better understanding of classwork
- Verification of skill mastery
- Corrective exercises in specific skills
- Homework activity directed to specific reading needs
- Practice for mastery
- Optimal use of teacher time

The exercises can be photocopied just as they appear for classroom use.
Complete answer keys for activities in this unit are provided on pages 269–289.

VOCABULARY   **A. Word Recognition**   1. *Uses context clues*
                                                  a. How the word is used in a
                                                     sentence

DIRECTIONS: Read the following sentences carefully. Circle the correct definition for the underlined word in each sentence.

1. <u>Demonstrators</u> circling in front of the plant wanted everyone to know that they wanted it closed.

   a. people who show how   b. people who protest   c. people who prove
                                                                something

2. <u>Evidence</u> must show that a drug will work before it is approved to be sold.

   a. a sign   b. proof   c. experiments

3. To win in contests of knowledge and skill, <u>exactitude</u> and promptitude are necessary.

   a. being precise and   b. speed   c. memory
      accurate

4. A head cold can make a voice sound <u>nasal</u>.

   a. hoarse   b. choked   c. as if coming through the
                                                     nose

5. Ruth was taken by surprise and her breath <u>caught</u> suddenly in her throat.

   a. was received   b. gave her a choking   c. understood
                          sensation

6. Although it was <u>weathered</u> by long months of sun and storms and sea, the ship was beautiful.

   a. affected by exposure   b. endured   c. changed

7. I turned and saw a group of men <u>surging</u> toward me.

   a. walking in the usual   b. rushing as a mob   c. rising
      way

8. The little boys studied the stranger for a moment and then <u>cautiously</u> smiled.

   a. bravely   b. fearlessly   c. carefully and timidly

9. The children rarely saw strangers. They were <u>reluctant</u> to approach us.

   a. unwilling   b. disposed   c. eager

10. It was a very quiet ride home with each one of us lost in private <u>reverie</u>.

   a. conversation   b. deep thought   c. delight

VOCABULARY **A. Word Recognition** 1. *Uses context clues*
                                        a. How the word is used in a
                                           sentence

DIRECTIONS: Read each sentence carefully. Circle the word that gives the meaning of the underlined word or phrase.

1. When I am in high school, I shall visit the grounds of the colleges so that I can decide which one to attend.

   a. stadiums   b. arenas   c. campuses

2. The display of fireworks was vivid, striking, and impressive.

   a. noisy   b. spectacular   c. full of noise and color

3. "Rousing, encouraging, exciting" were the words used by the travelers to describe their fellow travelers.

   a. stimulating   b. cool   c. animated

4. Some of the old cities of Europe are pleasingly odd and unusual in appearance.

   a. not ordinary   b. weird   c. quaint

5. The Canadian and American Rockies are considered as having pleasing and beautiful scenery.

   a. tourist   b. scenic   c. awesome

6. Great achievements by persons of advanced age have proven that ability has no limit in time.

   a. is ageless   b. is ancient   c. is antique

7. You did not have to answer all of the questions on the test. Some were to be answered only if you chose them.

   a. optional   b. unnecessary   c. easy

8. Miss Jones, our arithmetic teacher, trained us to form an opinion of a possible answer to a problem.

   a. compute   b. estimate   c. be precise

9. Airplanes, trains, and buses are different kinds of transportation that we can use.

   a. employ   b. prefer   c. wear out

10. The mountains where the Winter Olympics were held were of a beauty that took our breath away.

    a. frightening   b. breathtaking   c. awesome

VOCABULARY   A. Word Recognition   1. *Uses context clues*
                                        a. How the word is used in a
                                            sentence

DIRECTIONS: Read the following sentences carefully. Circle the correct definition for the underlined word or phrase in each sentence.

1. After playing in the ocean, the children came back to the picnic with ravenous appetites.

   a. raving   b. very small   c. very hearty

2. Most of what we know about ancient times has been learned because of the work done by archeologists.

   a. people who build   b. people who research   c. people who study the
      arches   and study ruins   human race
                                from antiquity

3. Abraham Lincoln, John F. Kennedy, and Dr. Martin Luther King all died as the result of assassination.

   a. disease   b. murder   c. accident

4. If a very sick person weathers the crisis of the illness, he or she will recover.

   a. states of the   b. withstands; gets the   c. is affected by
      atmosphere   better of

5. As they entered the theater, John checked his hat and coat but Linda kept her coat with her.

   a. paid by check   b. left with the   c. looked after;
                             attendant   watched

6. The daughter of the president broke a bottle of champagne against the ship and said, "I christen you 'Arizona.'"

   a. give you the name   b. test your construction   c. toast you

7. After the accident, Liza remained in a coma for a month.

   a. hospital   b. private room   c. unconscious state

8. "Come now, don't be idle," the old lady said to the new maid.

   a. remain without   b. keep working   c. keep the motor
      working   running

9. Specially arranged tours combine extensive travel with visits to many college and university campuses.

   a. time-consuming   b. far-reaching   c. costly

VOCABULARY   A. Word Recognition   1. *Uses context clues*
                                               a. How the word is used in a
                                                  sentence

DIRECTIONS: Read the following sentences carefully. Circle the correct definition for the underlined word or phrase in each sentence.

1. During some seasons earthquakes, floods, volcanic eruptions, tornadoes, and hurricanes abound.

    a. happen   b. exist   c. occur in great number

2. People who came to celebrate the one-week festival lived in temporary huts made of branches.

    a. fragile   b. not permanent   c. near the temple

3. The Peace Corps volunteer, hard-headed and resolute, kept at his work even when it seemed he would fail.

    a. determined   b. fixed   c. ambitious

4. Wherever there is hardship, be it hunger, pain, or want, we must try to alleviate it.
    a. lessen   b. erase   c. cure

5. The floor of the cabin sagged dangerously, preventing anything placed on it from staying put.

    a. leaned to one side   b. was bumpy   c. was slippery

6. The mobile home had no underpinning; it sat flat on the ground.

    a. foundation   b. wheels   c. lashing with cords

7. The Urban League's Work Ethic Program for teenage summer employment has stringent attendance and performance rules.

    a. with strings attached   b. strict   c. strained

8. One excused absence from work would mean termination of your job.

    a. quitting   b. being limited in   c. being fired from

9. "Being hungry," in the sense of wanting something very badly, is the best incentive for succeeding. There is no pill or injection for it.

    a. procedure   b. spur   c. motivation

10. It was a dark and blustery night. Father was hunched over the steering wheel trying to keep the car on the road.

    a. was bent with rounded   b. was punching with his   c. had a feeling
       back   fist or elbow

VOCABULARY   A. Word Recognition   1. *Uses context clues*
                                         b. Function of the word

---

DIRECTIONS: Circle the best definition for the underlined word in each sentence.

1. Coach Santilli made the point that a body in top physical condition is an athlete's best asset.

    a. mark; dot   b. remark; statement of   c. direction
                             an important idea

2. To revive the dying fire, one of the campers poked it.

    a. extinguished   b. jabbed   c. slowed

3. "We need the rest of the dessert for tonight," Mother said. "Don't you dare polish it off!"

    a. shine   b. wax   c. finish

4. People in a county neighboring ours are opposed to the building of a new highway.

    a. next to   b. close by   c. far away from

5. Because he held the compass upside down, the needle led him in the wrong direction.

    a. sewing tool   b. compass pointer   c. tease

6. Natural foods are better for your health.

    a. vegetable   b. animal   c. not artificial

7. The Barber Shop Quartet sang about horse and buggy days and about the old nag, the old gray mare.

    a. poor horse   b. witch   c. scold

8. "That's a new angle," commented the teacher when she heard Eileen's excuse for being late.

    a. corner   b. math figure   c. slant

VOCABULARY   A. Word Recognition   1. *Uses context clues*
                                      b. Function of the word

DIRECTIONS: Circle the best definition for the underlined word or phrase in each sentence.

1. The frame of mind with which you face life can make you or break you.
   a. picture   b. attitude   c. framework

2. Senator Quagmire insisted that he had the floor and would not yield it.
   a. bottom surface   b. right to address the   c. silence
                                  assembly

3. When boys tease and punch each other, it often ends in a fray.
   a. brawl   b. broken bone   c. having to be separated

4. Many retired people are said to be on a fixed income because they do not receive pay
   increases from time to time as people who are working do.
   a. tampered   b. resolute   c. unchanging

5. People who get angry easily are said to have a short fuse.
   a. protective device   b. mix; blend with others   c. bad temper

6. The kidnappers had gagged their victim.
   a. played a trick on   b. placed something in   c. taken away the freedom
                                  the mouth of   of discussion of

7. The trees were left iced by the storm of freezing rain.
   a. as blocks of ice   b. supplied with ice   c. as if frosted like a cake

8. About two years ago, stores were flooded with "Pet Rocks."
   a. deep in water   b. overflowing   c. overstocked

9. He was a sailor and his thin, wiry figure made it easy for him to climb the rigging.
   a. made of wire   b. stiff   c. lean and strong

VOCABULARY   A. Word Recognition   1. *Uses context clues*
                                       b. Function of the word

DIRECTIONS: Circle the best definition for the underlined word or phrase in each sentence.

1. The fortifications appeared bare and ugly.
   a. unclothed   b. unadorned; plain   c. insufficient

2. In a lumberyard, the odor of raw new lumber stirs the imagination.
   a. uncooked   b. cold and damp   c. natural

3. Although they were fine mountain climbers, they looked with awe at the forbidding slope.
   a. opposing   b. difficult to climb   c. preventing

4. As soon as the twins gave their excuse for being late, they felt a cloud of suspicion over them.
   a. overcast   b. atmosphere   c. defect

5. She froze in her tracks when she heard him yell, "Wait!"
   a. stopped   b. congealed   c. hardened

6. They were taken aback by the girl's prompt action.
   a. pressed back   b. made uneasy   c. turned back

7. When he was touched by humor, a peculiar quirk overtook the old man's usually stern mouth.
   a. mannerism   b. study   c. stroke

8. The cliff jutted out over the ocean.
   a. stood out   b. hung   c. jumped up

9. The empty warehouse was a cavernous structure.
   a. vast   b. hollow   c. underground

VOCABULARY   **A. Word Recognition**   **1. *Uses context clues***
                                                   b. Function of the word

DIRECTIONS: Circle the best definition for the underlined word or phrase in each sentence.

1. The biggest department store was closed because the clerks were taking stock.

    a. taking inventory   b. selling shares   c. taking cuttings

2. Coddled eggs are preferred by the English.

    a. pampered   b. cooked by standing   c. scrambled
                                      in hot water

3. It was a quirk of fate that we missed the plane that crashed.

    a. twist   b. quip   c. chance

4. You missed the point of the joke by not listening carefully.

    a. remark   b. mark; dot   c. focus

5. Fortunately, Tom had a good sense of humor because his friends gave him the needle mercilessly.

    a. gave him the   b. gave him the   c. teased
       sewing tool   compass pointer

6. Champagne is not a still wine.

    a. hushed   b. sparkling   c. motionless

7. The comedian made tart remarks to his noisy audience.

    a. sour   b. cutting   c. fruity

8. Greta will have to polish the silver for the party.

    a. shine   b. wax   c. finish

9. You simply must learn the difference between acute and obtuse angles.

    a. corners   b. slants   c. geometric figures

10. Cakes are usually iced in white for weddings.

    a. covered with ice   b. covered with frosting   c. made of ice

VOCABULARY   **A. Word Recognition**   **2.** *Uses configuration clues*
                                         a. Visual impressions of words

DIRECTIONS: Look at the pictures carefully. Match each picture with a descriptive word by writing the letter of the picture on the line next to the word.

a.

b.

c.
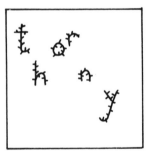

d.

e.

_____ 1. smiling

_____ 2. crowded

_____ 3. tense

_____ 4. thorny

_____ 5. puzzled

_____ 6. snarled

_____ 7. head, leader

_____ 8. imprisoned

_____ 9. joker

_____ 10. helpless

f.

g.

h.
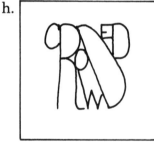

i.

j.
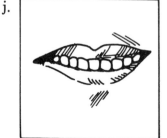

VOCABULARY   A. Word Recognition   2. *Uses configuration clues*
a. Visual impressions of words

DIRECTIONS: Look at the pictures carefully. Match each picture with a descriptive word by writing the letter of the picture on the line provided next to the word.

a.

_____ 1. wilted

_____ 2. shrinking violet

f.

b.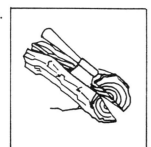

_____ 3. spatter

_____ 4. odd

g.

c.

_____ 5. dangling

_____ 6. cradled

h.

d.

_____ 7. splitting

_____ 8. leftover

i.

e.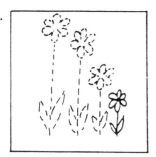

_____ 9. shapeless

_____ 10. musical

j.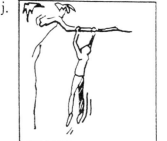

VOCABULARY   A. Word Recognition   **2. *Uses configuration clues***
                                    a. Visual impressions of words

DIRECTIONS: Look at the pictures carefully. Match each picture with a descriptive word by putting the letter of the picture on the space provided next to the word.

a.

f.

_____ 1. smug

_____ 2. tepid

b.

g.

_____ 3. grumpy

_____ 4. flowery

c.

h.

_____ 5. self-control

_____ 6. chiseled

d.

i.

_____ 7. gentle

_____ 8. sticky

e.

j.

_____ 9. checkered

_____ 10. firmly

Name: _____ Date: _____

VOCABULARY   A. Word Recognition   2. *Uses configuration clues*
                                     a. Visual impressions of words

DIRECTIONS: Look at the pictures carefully. Match each picture with a descriptive expression by putting the letter of the picture on the space provided next to the expression.

a.

_____ 1. "bombs bursting in air"

f.
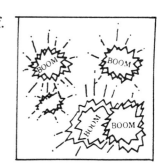

_____ 2. heavy hand

b.

_____ 3. stifled

g.

_____ 4. diamond-paned window

c.

_____ 5. eyes lighted up

h.

_____ 6. cost an arm and a leg

d.

_____ 7. dog tag

i.
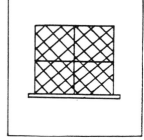

_____ 8. a bite to eat

e.
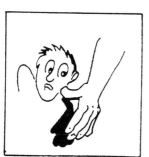

_____ 9. No way!

j.

_____ 10. He found himself the target ...

VOCABULARY   **A. Word Recognition**   **2. *Uses configuration clues***
                   b. Shape, length of words

DIRECTIONS: Match each word in column A with the correct configuration in column B.

A.   **B.**

1. _____ roller
2. _____ gems
3. _____ individual
4. _____ swarm
5. _____ shattered
6. _____ stoop
7. _____ spitball
8. _____ hardwood
9. _____ faded
10. _____ communism
11. _____ appreciate
12. _____ entertain
13. _____ research
14. _____ woolen
15. _____ taxpayer
16. _____ head-on
17. _____ emperor
18. _____ mountains
19. _____ sponsor
20. _____ classroom

VOCABULARY   A. Word Recognition   2. *Uses configuration clues*
                                        b. Shape, length of words

DIRECTIONS: Read each sentence carefully. Look at the word configuration and write in the word that is missing.

1. The _____ children were restless, noisy, and could not sit still.

2. The _____ of Independence is celebrated on July 4.

3. After his _____ from the army, Paul decided to go to college.

4. His bullets were spent, so the sheriff threw away his gun and punched with his _____ .

5. The more _____ my blue jeans, the better I like them.

6. _____ shouted the policeman at the fleeing thief.

7. As a result of research, cancer now is often _____ .

8. Andy _____ his shoulder playing football.

9. For Halloween, we stuffed a _____ that looked like a witch.

10. At the beginning of the show, the children sang, "Let us _____ you."

11. How can I _____ my thanks?

12. Taxpayers _____ a refund.

Name: _____ Date: _____

DIRECTIONS: Read each sentence carefully. Look at the word configuration and write in the word that is missing.

1. If you want money for your car, you will have to ⬚⬚⬚ for a job.

2. Milk and milk products give the body much needed ⬚⬚⬚ .

3. Sodium chloride is ⬚⬚⬚ called salt.

4. ⬚⬚⬚ was the form of government in Russia.

5. Being ⬚⬚⬚ is merely showing concern and consideration for others.

6. Professional baseball players, basketball players, and football players sometimes hold out before signing a ⬚⬚⬚ .

7. In order to work faster, the house painter used a ⬚⬚⬚ instead of a brush.

8. My friend looks at life with a very cheerful, happy ⬚⬚⬚ .

9. Napoleon was an ⬚⬚⬚ .

10. Before school in the morning, the band practices playing and marching in ⬚⬚⬚ .

11. The sixth grade mixed chorus sang ⬚⬚⬚ well.

12. Diamonds, rubies, sapphires, and pearls are all ⬚⬚⬚ .

VOCABULARY   A. Word Recognition   2. *Uses configuration clues*
                                      b. Shape, length of words

DIRECTIONS: Read each sentence carefully. Look at the word configuration and write the word that is missing.

1. A father and his children belong to different ⬚⬚⬚⬚⬚⬚⬚⬚⬚⬚⬚ .

2. Very few victims walk away from ⬚⬚⬚⬚-⬚⬚ collisions.

3. Each child is an ⬚⬚⬚⬚⬚⬚⬚ unique and different.

4. As editor of the *Edwardsville Evening Paper*, John is following a career as a ⬚⬚⬚⬚⬚⬚⬚⬚⬚⬚ .

5. Abn bel Saud worships Allah; that makes him a ⬚⬚⬚⬚⬚ .

6. Holland is not noted for mountains but for its ⬚⬚⬚⬚⬚⬚⬚ .

7. Today, our mothers buy fabric by the yard; we will buy it by the ⬚⬚⬚⬚ .

8. Getting oil by drilling off the coast is called ⬚⬚⬚⬚⬚⬚⬚⬚ drilling.

9. Thomas Edison is said to have had more ⬚⬚⬚⬚⬚⬚⬚ for his inventions than anyone else.

10. The doctor telephoned the ⬚⬚⬚⬚⬚⬚⬚⬚ for a prescription.

11. For Americans, the ⬚⬚⬚⬚⬚ is a measure of weight; for the English, it is money.

12. Gold has always been one of the most ⬚⬚⬚⬚⬚⬚⬚⬚ metals.

VOCABULARY   **A. Word Recognition**   **3. *Uses language rhythms***
                                           a. Rhyming clues

DIRECTIONS: Read each group of words below. Cross out the words that do not rhyme. If none of the words rhyme, write <u>none</u>. If all of the words rhyme, write <u>all</u>.

1.	powers	hours	ours	flowers	_____
2.	hearth	earth	birth	bath	_____
3.	snows	prose	toes	glows	_____
4.	tire	tear	fear	here	_____
5.	pain	skin	dim	gun	_____
6.	ye	sea	flee	tee	_____
7.	loan	stone	bone	boon	_____
8.	fey	fee	gray	they	_____
9.	cry	merrily	sigh	die	_____
10.	flow	flaw	flue	flee	_____

VOCABULARY   A. Word Recognition   3. *Uses language rhythms*
                                                       a. Rhyming clues

DIRECTIONS: Read each group of words below. Cross out the words that do not rhyme. If none of the words rhyme, write <u>none</u>. If all of the words rhyme, write <u>all</u>.

1.	nutty	butter	putty	rutty	_____
2.	text	fact	pert	pest	_____
3.	lost	post	toast	host	_____
4.	oar	soar	sour	more	_____
5.	fright	might	sight	light	_____
6.	hockey	jockey	jocko	perky	_____
7.	lonesome	winsome	wholesome	fulsome	_____
8.	witch	which	pitch	ditch	_____
9.	whirl	whorl	world	wurley	_____
10.	hoot	foot	shoot	root	_____
11.	food	mood	brood	rood	_____
12.	coil	pearl	foil	boil	_____

VOCABULARY   A. Word Recognition   3. *Uses language rhythms*
                                       a. Rhyming clues

DIRECTIONS: Read each group of words below. Underline the pair of words in each group that rhyme.

1.	vanity	sanity	reality	history
2.	thrust	boast	toast	foist
3.	old	foal	foil	cold
4.	puddle	puzzle	nozzle	nuzzle
5.	flutter	mother	shutter	porter
6.	dawdle	middle	fiddle	waddle
7.	charity	parity	poetry	cavity
8.	prudent	bent	student	study
9.	asp	waist	cast	fast
10.	flat	eight	ate	what
11.	jazz	maze	raise	razz
12.	hockey	joker	jockey	porky

VOCABULARY   A. **Word Recognition**   3. *Uses language rhythms*
                                            a. Rhyming clues

DIRECTIONS: Circle the pair of words in each group that have two rhyming syllables.

1.	furry	dreary	cheery	sorry
2.	clinging	sighing	setting	forgetting
3.	jealousy	weary	beauty	duty
4.	stifling	zealous	rifling	arduous
5.	happily	merrily	verily	fully
6.	backing	baking	looking	raking

DIRECTIONS: Underline the pair of words in each group that rhyme:

7.	coax	ox	stock	fox
8.	moan	lone	gone	moon
9.	come	comb	bomb	dome
10.	broad	road	applaud	clothes
11.	tuned	zoned	toned	bond
12.	soccer	poker	taker	locker

VOCABULARY   A. Word Recognition   3. *Uses language rhythms*
                                     b. Appreciation for general rhythm
                                        of well-expressed ideas

DIRECTIONS: Read the following phrases. From each pair, select and underline the phrase that has rhythm and best expresses the idea.

	A	B
1.	a group of housetops	a huddle of housetops
2.	boats drifting to rest	boats coming in
3.	a parade passing	waving flags and beating drums
4.	sick and tired of everything	weary of words and people
5.	a symphony of words	nice-sounding words
6.	not a noise around	stillness answered
7.	the sky, a cloudy sea	the cloudy sky
8.	the silent house	the house, lonely and still
9.	to be attracted	to feel its call, to feel its lure
10.	well-kept lawns	the lawns close-shaven
11.	the falling fire to tend	to stoke the fire going out
12.	her delight, the tree's shady height	she loved the tall tree

VOCABULARY   A. Word Recognition   **3. *Uses language rhythms***
                                     b. Appreciation for general rhythm
                                         of well-expressed ideas

DIRECTIONS: Match the ordinary phrase with the one that expresses the same idea better and with rhythm. Place the letter in the blank provided.

_____	1. the sea that doesn't stop	a. in the winter of his life
_____	2. time flies	b. waste not your hour
_____	3. an old grandpa	c. the roaming, restless sea
_____	4. the bay flows into the ocean	d. when my mind was seized by fancy
_____	5. don't waste time	e. Father Time a sprinter is
_____	6. when I daydreamed	f. where the bay into the ocean spills
_____	7. the first violets appear	g. the boat spun round and round
_____	8. the boat kept turning	h. the ship went down like lead
_____	9. the ship sank fast	i. feathers of incense fly
_____	10. incense rising	j. the surf boiled white
_____	11. the rough swell of the sea	k. billowing clouds
_____	12. clouds growing bigger	l. newborn violets bloom

Name: _____ Date: _____

VOCABULARY   A. Word Recognition   **3. *Uses language rhythms***
                                     b. Appreciation for general rhythm
                                     of well-expressed ideas

DIRECTIONS: Read the following phrases. Indicate with an X the phrases that have rhythm and express an idea well. Mark with an O the phrases that do not have rhythm and do not express an idea well.

_____	1.	girl with tresses flaxen
_____	2.	tulips bursting into bloom
_____	3.	the sky a cloudy sea
_____	4.	the grass in May
_____	5.	time seemed endless
_____	6.	I like to couch me in the hay
_____	7.	a man of holiness, a man of hope, a man of joy
_____	8.	the fluttering, sputtering of the spray
_____	9.	the snow-bound mountain
_____	10.	shadows twining and twisting

Name: _____ Date: _____

VOCABULARY   A. Word Recognition   3. *Uses language rhythms*
                                        b. Appreciation for general rhythm
                                           of well-expressed ideas

_____

DIRECTIONS: Read the following phrases. Indicate with an X the phrases that have rhythm and express an idea well. Mark with an O the phrases that do not have rhythm and do not express an idea well.

_____	1.	elevators going up
_____	2.	people of all ages
_____	3.	the whining, moaning, lonely wind
_____	4.	where the brooklet into the river spills
_____	5.	a stuffed Spanish olive
_____	6.	days in dull succession
_____	7.	clover weeping the dew
_____	8.	daisies bowing to the wind
_____	9.	idle moments
_____	10.	night came early

VOCABULARY   B. Knows and Uses Prefixes and Suffixes

DIRECTIONS: The following words have either a prefix or a suffix, and some have both. Circle the root word in each one.

1.	unspeakable	8.	injustice	15.	prediction
2.	semiweekly	9.	magician	16.	statement
3.	heroic	10.	unpatriotic	17.	unemotional
4.	administrator	11.	cowardice	18.	wealthy
5.	classify	12.	disillusion	19.	lifeless
6.	coverage	13.	maiden	20.	spiteful
7.	deduction	14.	politician		

DIRECTIONS: Select and write in the space provided the suffix that will give the correct meaning for the following root words.

21. content   _____   state of being content
    -ness   -hood   -ment

22. nervous   _____   state of being nervous
    -ness   -ous   -ment

23. sleep   _____   being without sleep
    -less   -hood   -full

24. eat   _____   capable of being eaten
    -able   -ible   -ive

25. danger   _____   abounding in danger
    -ness   -ous   -ant

26. sea   _____   toward the direction of the sea
    -hood   -ward   -some

27. man   _____   state of being a man
    -hood   -ion   -ance

28. joy   _____   full of joy
    -ness   -ful   -ic

29. act   _____   one who acts
    -er   -or   -an

30. Arab   _____   like the Arab
    -y   -ic   -ice

VOCABULARY   **B. Knows and Uses Prefixes and Suffixes**

DIRECTIONS: Place a prefix before the root word to create a word with the definition given.

1. _____ code   to figure out a secret meaning from

2. _____ agree   to quarrel, not to agree

3. _____ just   change to fit

4. _____ mature   not mature

5. _____ mediate   in the middle, between low and high

6. _____ spell   to spell wrongly

7. _____ regular   unusual, not regular

8. _____ sense   foolishness, not making sense

9. _____ fine   extra fine, over the ordinary

10. _____ like   different, not like

DIRECTIONS: Select and write in the space provided the prefix that will give the correct meaning for the following root words.

11. _____ cycle   to return for further use, to use again
                               re-   tri-   bi-

12. _____ assemble   to take apart
                               dis-   post-   ab-

13. _____ navigate   to sail around
                               inter-   ante-   circum-

14. _____ flate   to let the air from
                               dis-   de-   ab-

15. _____ link   to connect between
                               inter-   ante-   circum-

16. _____ pronounce   to say wrongly
                               dis-   mis-   in-

17. _____ condition   to repair, to put in use again
                               per-   pre-   re-

18. _____ ject   to throw forward
                               pre-   per-   pro-

19. _____ man   above human
                               per-   super-   semi-

20. _____ circle   half circle
                               post-   peri-   semi-

VOCABULARY   **B. Knows and Uses Prefixes and Suffixes**

DIRECTIONS: Add a suffix to each root word to create a word with the meaning given.

1. port   _____   capable of being carried

2. refer   _____   something in the state of being referred to for information

3. value   _____   without value

4. state   _____   act of saying or writing something

5. econom   _____   to make economies; to save

6. equip   _____   state of being a supply necessary for a particular service or sport

7. light   _____   in a light way

8. home   _____   turning to home

9. weak   _____   in a weak way

10. wax   _____   like wax

DIRECTIONS: Underline the suffix in each of the following words. Then draw a line to its correct meaning.

11. requirement   a. without sight; blind

12. finalize   b. something that is needed

13. eastward   c. made of wool

14. sightless   d. in a proud way

15. proudly   e. to make definite, to make final

16. warmly   f. in a complete way

17. organizer   g. in the direction of the east

18. elector   h. one who votes

19. completely   i. in a kind, warm way

20. woolen   j. one who plans and arranges things

VOCABULARY   **B. Knows and Uses Prefixes and Suffixes**

DIRECTIONS: Write the root word, its prefix or suffix, and the meaning of the prefix or suffix on the lines under the correct headings.

		Prefix	Root Word	Suffix	Meaning
1.	biform	_____	_____	_____	_____
2.	defrost	_____	_____	_____	_____
3.	trusty	_____	_____	_____	_____
4.	truthful	_____	_____	_____	_____
5.	disapprove	_____	_____	_____	_____
6.	metallic	_____	_____	_____	_____
7.	circumscribe	_____	_____	_____	_____
8.	liquefy	_____	_____	_____	_____
9.	purity	_____	_____	_____	_____
10.	degrade	_____	_____	_____	_____
11.	bumpy	_____	_____	_____	_____
12.	misspell	_____	_____	_____	_____
13.	sanity	_____	_____	_____	_____
14.	intercom	_____	_____	_____	_____
15.	exhale	_____	_____	_____	_____
16.	poetic	_____	_____	_____	_____
17.	shaken	_____	_____	_____	_____
18.	predict	_____	_____	_____	_____
19.	postscript	_____	_____	_____	_____
20.	primary	_____	_____	_____	_____

VOCABULARY   **C. Word Meaning**   **1.** *Knows multiple meanings of words*

DIRECTIONS: The underlined word in each sentence has several meanings. Draw a circle around the best meaning for each sentence.

1. On the night before the elections, the candidates spoke at a <u>rally</u>.
   a. bring to order again   b. mass meeting   c. partial recovery

2. To <u>further</u> her career, the actress did many things.
   a. at a greater distance   b. additional   c. help along

3. The <u>fund</u> for the John Jay Scholarship was increased by new contributions.
   a. sum of money   b. supply   c. to change to a long-term debit

4. Who won the game? Nobody. It was a <u>tie</u>.
   a. connection   b. equal score   c. necktie

5. The mountain <u>slide</u> had crossed the path.
   a. fallen earth and rock   b. picture for projection   c. glass for a microscope

6. After the accident, John had <u>major</u> surgery.
   a. most important   b. army officer   c. field of study

7. His Marine Corps training was evident in the <u>fold</u> in his trousers.
   a. bend in sections   b. fail in business   c. crease

8. The use of dynamite is for <u>general</u> blasting.
   a. high officer   b. common or widespread   c. indefinite

9. Alice looked at herself in the <u>glass</u>.
   a. container for drinking   b. mirror   c. breakable material

10. Some woods, like oak and maple, are <u>hard</u>.
    a. not easy   b. without sympathy   c. solid, tough

VOCABULARY   C. Word Meaning   1. *Knows multiple meanings of words*

DIRECTIONS: The underlined word in each sentence has several meanings. Draw a circle around the best meaning for each sentence.

1. By taking advantage of the helpless man, he proved he was a <u>heel</u>.
   a. back part of the foot   b. end crust of bread   c. bad person

2. People with little or no money find the cost of living <u>high</u>.
   a. above others   b. expensive   c. noble

3. Before you give orders, learn to <u>mind</u> them.
   a. obey   b. care   c. brains

4. I much prefer <u>natural</u> foods.
   a. formed by nature   b. true to life   c. not fake

5. On highways, radar is used to <u>time</u> automobiles.
   a. choose the moment for   b. measure speed of   c. when things happen

6. It is sad not to <u>trust</u> anyone.
   a. have faith in   b. expect, hope   c. an honorable duty

7. Our names were called in alphabetical <u>order</u>.
   a. to command   b. amount bought   c. arrangement

8. A currently popular <u>instrument</u> is the guitar.
   a. tool   b. document   c. object to make music

9. Burt and Kurt had trucks for <u>hire</u>.
   a. rent   b. to give a job   c. to put up

10. To say that something is "down in the <u>hollow</u>" suggests there are hills or mountains around.
    a. empty   b. bowl-shaped   c. valley

Name: _____ Date: _____

VOCABULARY   C. Word Meaning   1. *Knows multiple meanings of words*

DIRECTIONS: The underlined word in each sentence has several meanings. Draw a circle around the best meaning for each sentence.

1. When I meet the stranger, how shall I know him?
   a. recognize   b. understand   c. be skilled in

2. The river that flows through town was at flood level.
   a. the height of   b. even   c. as high as

3. We have a census to number the people.
   a. count   b. how many   c. quite a few

4. After he had bought the car, he felt he had been soaked for it.
   a. let stand in water   b. gotten very wet   c. charged too much

5. 'Tis the season to be jolly.
   a. spring, summer, fall, or winter   b. add salt and pepper   c. time for certain sports or events

6. For a week after the big storm, we were without power.
   a. control of authority   b. the ability to act   c. electricity

7. Many persons have done silly things just to be in the Guinness Book of World Records.
   a. phonograph disks   b. scores never reached before   c. books of past happenings

8. Although he is only twelve years of age, Jim is quite independent.
   a. thinks for himself   b. free   c. on his own

9. One thing I dislike about summer is the ticks.
   a. blood-sucking insects   b. check marks   c. sounds of a clock

10. Bill, the watchmaker, said that the spring was broken.
    a. March, April, May   b. flow of water from the earth   c. part to be wound

VI

VOCABULARY   C. Word Meaning   1. *Knows multiple meanings of words*

DIRECTIONS: The underlined word in each sentence has several meanings. Draw a circle around the best meaning for each sentence.

1. Luke prefers <u>hot</u> mustard.
   a. very spicy   b. very warm   c. jazzy

2. Unfortunately, the teacher could not <u>interest</u> the students.
   a. have a liking for   b. share   c. have the power to hold attention

3. Field days are held in the <u>open</u>.
   a. clear   b. out-of-doors   c. not shut

4. "<u>Out</u>!" cried the umpire.
   a. baseball play call   b. into the open   c. off

5. The Supreme Court Justice served as a <u>page</u> in his youth.
   a. messenger   b. printed piece of paper   c. call over loudspeaker

6. To celebrate her coronation, the new queen granted <u>pardons</u>.
   a. forgivenesses   b. excuses   c. freedom for criminals

7. The dignified English lady asked for a <u>spot</u> of tea.
   a. little bit   b. dirty stain   c. place

8. The pitcher, very alert, did not let anyone <u>steal</u>.
   a. rob   b. sneak a base   c. big bargain

9. We had to <u>stack</u> the wood so that it would be ready for winter.
   a. pile up   b. a large amount   c. a chimney

10. Distance <u>lends</u> enchantment.
    a. gives a quality of   b. loans   c. furnishes

VOCABULARY   C. Word Meaning   2. *Can associate words and feelings*

DIRECTIONS: Read each line carefully. Then cross out the word that <u>does</u> <u>not</u> express the feeling of the first word.

1.	mournful	unhappy	awake	sad	sorrowful
2.	peevish	amiable	irritable	cross	fretful
3.	affectionate	loving	tender	warm	affected
4.	haughty	vain	proud	high	scornful
5.	surly	bad-tempered	abrupt	certain	rude
6.	querulous	whining	content	complaining	quarrelsome
7.	abashed	burned	ashamed	uneasy	embarrassed
8.	earnest	determined	eager	serious	frivolous
9.	melancholy	sad	happy	low-spirited	gloomy
10.	rebellious	disobedient	unruly	defiant	submissive

VOCABULARY   C. Word Meaning   2. *Can associate words and feelings*

DIRECTIONS: Read each line carefully. Then cross out the word that <u>does</u> <u>not</u> express the feeling of the first word.

1.	amiable	friendly	rude	good-natured	agreeable
2.	leery	sly	wary	suspicious	afraid
3.	forlorn	deserted	abandoned	accompanied	sad
4.	hesitant	decisive	reluctant	unwilling	uncertain
5.	insignificant	small	important	meaningless	unimportant
6.	audacious	bold	daring	fearless	cowardly
7.	dubious	doubtful	hesitating	unclear	certain
8.	elated	happy	jubilant	depressed	in high spirits
9.	belligerent	pugnacious	fond of fighting	agreeable	quarrelsome
10.	serene	calm	disturbed	quiet	peaceful

VOCABULARY   C. Word Meaning   *2. Can associate words and feelings*

DIRECTIONS: Each word under column A describes a feeling. Match it with the word under column B that expresses each feeling.

A

_____ 1. elation	_____ 4. forbearance	
_____ 2. despair	_____ 5. indifference	
_____ 3. envy	_____ 6. rapture	

_____ 7. frustration	_____ 10. reverence
_____ 8. nonchalance	_____ 11. resentment
_____ 9. anguish	_____ 12. reluctance

_____ 13. shame	_____ 16. mercy
_____ 14. alarm	_____ 17. placidity
_____ 15. perplexity	_____ 18. prudence

B

a. patience
b. jealousy
c. dismay
d. happiness
e. unconcern
f. hopelessness
g. assurance
h. delight
i. arrogance
j. self-confidence
k. unwillingness
l. respect
m. coolness
n. suffering
o. disappointment
p. hurt
q. apathy
r. composure
s. disgrace
t. panic
u. confusion
v. caution
w. tranquility
x. clemency

VOCABULARY   C. Word Meaning   2. *Can associate words and feelings*

DIRECTIONS: Read the first word in each line and circle the word that expresses the feeling that the word denotes.

1. convinced	willing	unsure	hesitant	confident
2. gracious	graceful	kind	favoring	displeased
3. puzzled	ravaged	perplexed	vague	doubting
4. disgusted	offended	full	gorged	surfeited
5. exhausted	lost	wasted	worn out	reeking
6. secure	safe	tied	unsure	unguarded
7. frightened	timid	apprehensive	nervous	terrified
8. weary	weak	tired	uneasy	worm
9. indifferent	disliking	inattentive	uncaring	careless
10. dejected	rejected	dreary	downhearted	somber
11. irritated	uncomfortable	angry	sensitive	sore
12. repentant	glad	sorry	satisfied	unlamenting

VOCABULARY   C. Word Meaning   **3. *Formal and informal language***
                                   a. Identifies different speech patterns

DIRECTIONS: Match the underlined formal expression under A with its corresponding informal expression under B.

A

_____ 1. <u>The leader seems unaware that what he is saying doesn't make sense.</u>

_____ 2. Mrs. Buggs, who runs the boarding house, had boarders <u>who left without paying.</u>

_____ 3. Spear is the first official <u>to give the true facts.</u>

_____ 4. Arthur Mann, president of Majestic Motors, was recently <u>honored at a reception.</u>

_____ 5. <u>Vacation time is here.</u>

_____ 6. Patek is <u>the person in charge.</u>

_____ 7. <u>Examine your current situation realistically.</u>

_____ 8. She is always <u>unapproachable.</u>

_____ 9. Cynics say that superstars <u>perform only for the money.</u>

_____ 10. The best weapon in your <u>psychological arsenal is eating slowly.</u>

B

a. School's out!

b. given a big bash

c. Don't hog your food.

d. The guy is all wet.

e. to tell it like it is

f. are in show biz strictly for the big bucks

g. who were deadbeats

h. warm the bench

i. the big man

j. Look at the facts, man!

k. on her high horse

l. with clout

VOCABULARY   C. Word Meaning   **3. *Formal and informal language***
                                  a. Identifies different speech patterns

DIRECTIONS: In the space provided, write the formal equivalent for the underlined words or expressions below.

1. Joe received an <u>ID</u> bracelet for his birthday.

_____

2. If he acts <u>as if he owns the joint</u>, it's because he does.

_____

3. We asked the teacher to have a spelling <u>bee</u> the day before vacation.

_____

4. The performer was <u>plenty burned</u> when the audience kept talking during his act.

_____

5. When he did the same thing he had found fault with, <u>it was a horse of a different color.</u>

_____

6. The ex-president said that the newspaper's claim about what was uncontrollable was <u>a lot of baloney.</u>

_____

7. Mark <u>put the bite on his dad for fifty bucks.</u>

_____

8. Owning a car today will cost you <u>an arm and a leg.</u>

_____

9. What started as a friendly argument ended up in a <u>free-for-all.</u>

_____

10. No matter what it is, that woman always has to <u>run the show.</u>

_____

VOCABULARY   C. Word Meaning   3. *Formal and informal language*
                                   a. Identifies different speech patterns

DIRECTIONS: Read each of the following phrases or sentences carefully. On the line, write whether the expression is a <u>formal</u> or <u>colloquial</u> speech pattern.

1. To make fine hair appear thicker,
    try a tapered, layered cut.   _____

2. Old-fashioned apple cider vinegar
    is a great, inexpensive bath aid.   _____

3. Latest report fuels fat dispute.   _____

4. What a wet blanket!   _____

5. Office workers need to exercise.   _____

6. Don't back off before you give
    it the old one-two.   _____

7. Fran's grandma is afraid of
    creepy crawlers.   _____

8. Precise focusing brings out
    detail.   _____

9. I burned the midnight oil grinding
    out my report.   _____

10. We looked upon a scene of barren
    desolation.   _____

VOCABULARY   C. Word Meaning   3. *Formal and informal language*
                                  a. Identifies different speech patterns

DIRECTIONS: Read each of the following phrases or sentences carefully. On the line, write whether the expression is a <u>formal</u> or <u>colloquial</u> speech pattern.

_____   1. You can knock off the pose and act naturally now; the photographer scrammed twenty minutes ago.

_____   2. When photographing pets, use a fast shutter.

_____   3. Jeff stewed while he warmed the bench and his teammates made a splash.

_____   4. Most human beings, by nature and by necessity, are adaptable and learn to cope.

_____   5. The boss said, "You just ain't gonna get that raise you've been bellyaching about."

_____   6. Spear is the first guy to tell it like it is.

_____   7. A disquieting rumble sent everyone scurrying for safety.

_____   8. Riddle me this.

_____   9. Yanks crush Billy's gang.

_____   10. They called on me to speak.

VOCABULARY   C. Word Meaning   3. *Formal and informal language*
                                   b. Understands level of language usage

DIRECTIONS: Under column A is a list of situations. Under column B are formal and informal expressions. On the line, write the letter of the expression that would be correct for each situation.

		A		B

_____   1. The school bully is making threats ...

     a. I'll give you a fat lip.
     b. I shall mutilate your face.

_____   2. Miss Piggy's usual request ...

     a. Please get out of the way.
     b. Move it! Move it!

_____   3. A farmer catching kids stealing ...

     a. Please leave!
     b. Scram!

_____   4. A serious newspaper article ...

     a. Proponents of such issues are all wet.
     b. Proponents of such issues are misguided.

_____   5. A mother to her child ...

     a. Don't kid yourself, honey.
     b. Please do not deceive yourself.

_____   6. A very formal, strict, no-nonsense teacher to a pupil ...

     a. Don't try to bamboozle me!
     b. Your attempts at flattery will get you nowhere.

_____   7. Newspaperman to the President ...

     a. Mr. President, you don't truly mean that, do you?
     b. Aw, don't try to con us.

_____   8. You are thanking a person who has done you a favor although you do not know this person very well ...

     a. It sure helps to have friends with clout.
     b. It was kind of you to use your influence for me.

_____   9. Two boys fighting ...

     a. Please go away!
     b. Buzz off!

_____   10. Comedian doing his act ...

     a. Don't judge by appearances.
     b. What you see is what you get.

VOCABULARY   C. Word Meaning   3. *Formal and informal language*
                                   b. Understands level of language usage

DIRECTIONS: Under column A is a list of situations. Under column B are formal and informal expressions. On the line, write the letter of the expression that would be correct for each situation.

A   **B**

_____ 1. Happy students, bubbling   a. What an elegant party that
            over, leaving a party ...   was!
                                               b. What a bash!

_____ 2. Football player coming   a. We were creamed!
            home after losing a game,   b. Mother, we were very badly
            speaking to his mother ...   defeated.

_____ 3. You are writing a letter   a. Scrap that lousy plan!
            of protest to the mayor ...   b. Please consider abandoning
                                                   that unsound plan.

_____ 4. Boss of the road crew ...   a. Quit your bellyaching!
                                               b. Cease your complaining!

_____ 5. You are writing a letter   a. We bombed North in the finals.
            to your brother ...   b. We beat North with a wide
                                                   margin.

_____ 6. A reviewer of theater and   a. The play is a disaster.
            films in the newspaper ...   b. It stinks.

_____ 7. A letter asking for a   a. I'll tell it like it is.
            job ...   b. I shall inform you of the
                                                   circumstances.

_____ 8. An article in the business   a. They agreed to complete the
            section of the newspaper ...   merger.
                                               b. The companies gave their O.K.
                                                   to the deal.

_____ 9. A headline on the sports   a. Sugar's Brother Gets Nod
            page ...   b. Sugar's Brother Was Approved

_____ 10. Cheerleader at a pep   a. Come on gang! Let's go!
            rally ...   b. We hope a sizable number of
                                                   you will participate.

VOCABULARY   C. Word Meaning   *3. Formal and informal language*
                                               b. Understands level of language usage

DIRECTIONS: Read the following sentences. For the underlined portion, fill in the circle in front of the best meaning. If the expression underlined is a colloquial expression, select the more formal expression. If the expression underlined is a formal term, select the more colloquial expression.

1. When she arrived home after taking five hours for her usual thirty-minute trip, she exclaimed, "I'm beat!"
   - ○ a. "I was lost!"
   - ○ b. "I am exhausted!"
   - ○ c. "Someone beat me!"
   - ○ d. "My heart is pounding!"

2. Realizing the difficulty facing her, Bertha decided to take the bull by the horns.
   - ○ a. attack the problem fearlessly
   - ○ b. engage in a bull fight
   - ○ c. talk her way out of it
   - ○ d. have fun instead

3. The G.I. lost his dog tag.
   - ○ a. The sailor lost his sea bag.
   - ○ b. The marine lost his shoeshine set.
   - ○ c. The military man lost his way.
   - ○ d. The soldier lost his identification.

4. The whole kit and caboodle turned up for John's wedding.
   - ○ a. the cat and her kittens
   - ○ b. the rock band
   - ○ c. all the relatives
   - ○ d. a broken-down cab

5. Annoyed, she sent him away, saying, "Go fly a kite."
   - ○ a. "Go amuse yourself."
   - ○ b. "Stop bothering me."
   - ○ c. "I like kite-flying."
   - ○ d. "Be sure to come back."

6. When Bob imitated the teacher, he was so funny that we split our sides laughing.
   - ○ a. laughed with great abandon
   - ○ b. feared the teacher would come in
   - ○ c. laughed for awhile
   - ○ d. couldn't agree

7. Unfortunately, she couldn't care less about the consequences.
   - ○ a. was indifferent
   - ○ b. ought to be less worried
   - ○ c. ought to be more concerned
   - ○ d. ought to try harder

8. After visiting the scene of the disaster, the president spoke off the cuff about the problems he had observed.
   - ○ a. in a formal speech
   - ○ b. informally
   - ○ c. hitting his hand with his fist
   - ○ d. from notes he had made on his cuffs

VOCABULARY   C. Word Meaning   3. *Formal and informal language*
b. Understands level of language usage

DIRECTIONS: Read the following sentences. For the underlined portion, fill in the circle in front of the best meaning. If the expression underlined is a colloquial expression, select the more formal expression. If the expression underlined is a formal term, select the more colloquial expression.

1. Liza has gained so much weight, she is the size of a house.
   - a. square
   - b. plump
   - c. very overweight
   - d. dieting

2. Henry walks extremely carefully and gracefully.
   - a. like a boxer
   - b. like a dancer
   - c. like a tightrope walker
   - d. like a policeman

3. Dave drove slam-bang through the fence.
   - a. quietly
   - b. erratically
   - c. noisily
   - d. quickly and carelessly

4. A baseball player with a disposition to quarrel is likely to get into trouble with the umpire.
   - a. a chip on his shoulder
   - b. a broken bat
   - c. a bag of fried potatoes
   - d. an easy-going way

5. The poor fellow is so awkward and clumsy, it seems that things get broken if he only looks at them.
   - a. like the wind
   - b. like a bull in a china closet
   - c. like a bear
   - d. like a hurricane

6. When we arrived, we found them in the pool area soaking up the sun.
   - a. looking for shade
   - b. swimming in the sun
   - c. dodging the sun
   - d. sunbathing

7. "What a phony!" the children declared, sensing his deceit.
   - a. "How funny!"
   - b. "How can he do that?"
   - c. "What a fake!"
   - d. "He's not for real."

8. In a sympathetic manner, the judge said, "Tom, you will have to be examined by a shrink."
   - a. a pediatrist
   - b. a psychiatrist
   - c. an orthopedist
   - d. a neurologist

VOCABULARY   C. Word Meaning   4. *Distinguishes between aided and unaided recall*

DIRECTIONS: Read the following examples and indicate, by writing aided or unaided , the kind of recall described.

_____   1. After studying road maps of the region, Andy drove to the capital of the next state without having to look at a map.

_____   2. Miss Rose, the teacher, gave the students an open-book test.

_____   3. When she was twelve, Terry lost a spelling contest by spelling "embarrassment" wrong. After that, she always remembered that the word has two r's.

_____   4. Members of the armed forces are taught that if they are taken prisoner, they are to reveal only their name and serial number.

_____   5. When the bank teller asked him for his Social Security number, Raymond gave it to her from memory.

_____   6. When he decided to ask the girl he had met for a date, Charlie looked in his little black book for the telephone number she had given him.

_____   7. Before writing the word "receive," the student repeated to himself, "i before e except after c."

_____   8. After reading the test question, Isabella wrote down the word "track" because each letter stood for the important parts of the answer.

_____   9. When he found he had missed one bus, the traveler consulted the timetable for the departure time of the next one.

_____   10. If you "let your fingers do the walking" through the yellow pages of the telephone directory, you save time and effort.

VOCABULARY   C. Word Meaning   4. *Distinguishes between aided and unaided recall*

DIRECTIONS: Read the following sentences and indicate, by writing aided or unaided, the kind of recall described.

_____ 1. Albert consulted his program for the name of the attractive young actress.

_____ 2. The bank clerk had to look up Jim's account number because he did not know it.

_____ 3. The preacher did not consult his notes once during the sermon.

_____ 4. So you won't forget any item, take the grocery list with you.

_____ 5. Kevin found his mother's note to him on the family bulletin board and kept his appointment with the dentist.

_____ 6. Peggy did not pass the test. She had not studied because she had not taken notes.

_____ 7. Since Martin had recorded the interview on a cassette, he referred to it while writing his assignment.

_____ 8. During the assembly, the principal, as usual, addressed the students "off the cuff."

_____ 9. To make the best and most efficient use of your time and to achieve your goals, start each day by making out your agenda.

_____ 10. By referring to their itinerary, George and Roy were able to reconstruct their trip in detail.

VOCABULARY   C. Word Meaning   *4. Distinguishes between aided and unaided recall*

DIRECTIONS: Read the following sentences and indicate, by writing <u>aided</u> or <u>unaided</u>, the kind of recall described.

_____   1. "Did you get the license plate number?" the police officer asked the woman involved in the accident. "103-RZP, New York," she replied, hardly giving him time to finish.

_____   2. Dad consulted the newspaper again to find out what hours the new store would be open.

_____   3. She told me that the new poster store is across from the post office.

_____   4. While riding the bus downtown, Alice looked at their tickets again to make sure of the theater's location.

_____   5. Norman addressed the envelope the same way he had for years.

_____   6. The salesman quoted prices as if he were giving his own name.

_____   7. Although we kept coming back to the same place and were quite obviously lost, the driver would not take out his map.

_____   8. A photographic memory is a gift of great value but not necessarily when one is listening to a lecture.

_____   9. You don't need to look for your Social Security number when you make out your income tax report. It's on the form the government sends you.

_____ 10. "When did you change your oil last?" the mechanic asked. Dad answered quickly, "At twenty thousand miles."

VOCABULARY   C. Word Meaning   4. *Distinguishes between aided and unaided recall*

DIRECTIONS: Read the following examples and indicate, by writing <u>aided</u> or <u>unaided</u>, the kind of recall described.

_____   1. When she received a post card from Jeanne, Betty exclaimed, "Oh, I had forgotten all about her being on a trip!"

_____   2. As she left for her job in the morning, she put a note with the word "cleaners" on the visor of her car. When she returned home from work, she remembered to stop there.

_____   3. Christopher makes all of his contributions by check so that he will have a record of them.

_____   4. Why don't you look in the Entertainment section of the paper to see what is playing at the movies?

_____   5. He wanted to be sure the weather would be good, so he watched three different television weather forecasts.

_____   6. The Fourth of July always reminded Mary to send Rita a birthday card for the sixth.

_____   7. "I'll bet you can't name ten books you've read," Jeanne said to John. "Oh, yes I can," he replied. "Here's the card file where I keep a card for every book!"

_____   8. A metric converter is a handy gadget for someone who wants to convert yards to meters quickly.

_____   9. Donald's father sent him to the financial section of the newspaper to find out what the dollar was worth in Mexico.

_____   10. Greg's grandmother made a cake from scratch without even looking at a cookbook.

VOCABULARY   C. Word Meaning   5. *Can hyphenate words*

DIRECTIONS: Pretend that the words below are at the end of a line and must be hyphenated. Write each word in hyphenated form.

1. measure   _____

2. upturn   _____

3. perhaps   _____

4. accent   _____

5. mother   _____

6. forward   _____

7. sitting   _____

8. children   _____

9. police   _____

10. remain   _____

VOCABULARY   C. Word Meaning   *5. Can hyphenate words*

DIRECTIONS: Pretend that the words below are at the end of a line and must be hyphenated. Write each word in hyphenated form.

1. settle   _____

2. return   _____

3. quarter   _____

4. thoughtful   _____

5. explode   _____

6. coming   _____

7. lighthouse   _____

8. million   _____

9. almost   _____

10. certain   _____

VOCABULARY   C. Word Meaning   5. *Can hyphenate words*

DIRECTIONS: Pretend that the words below are at the end of a line and must be hyphenated. Write each word in hyphenated form.

1.   cannon   _____

2.   sculpture   _____

3.   vivid   _____

4.   tiny   _____

5.   starfish   _____

6.   wetness   _____

7.   marine   _____

8.   notebook   _____

9.   constant   _____

10. danger   _____

Name: _____ Date: _____

DIRECTIONS: Pretend that the words below are at the end of a line and must be hyphenated. Write each word in hyphenated form.

1.   today   _____

2.   person   _____

3.   childhood   _____

4.   hero   _____

5.   woman   _____

6.   wonder   _____

7.   fishing   _____

8.   parents   _____

9.   himself   _____

10. teaspoon   _____

VOCABULARY   C. Word Meaning   6. *Can provide synonyms*

DIRECTIONS: Cross out any word on a line which is <u>not</u> a synonym for the first word on that line.

1.	say	express	question	utter	state
2.	walk	stroll	step	stride	trudge
3.	cry	sob	shout	bawl	wail
4.	see	observe	notice	hide	detect
5.	death	life	decease	demise	passing
6.	give	donate	gift	provide	grant
7.	take	acquire	secure	get	obtain
8.	swallow	bird	gulp	drink	devour
9.	angry	irate	infuriated	enraged	mad
10.	redeem	ransom	free	liberate	rescue

VOCABULARY   C. Word Meaning   *6. Can provide synonyms*

DIRECTIONS: In the space provided, write a synonym for each underlined word in the sentences below.

_____   1. Dracula is really an ogre.

_____   2. What you need is a device to reduce time and effort.

_____   3. You will harvest what you sow.

_____   4. The musician needed deft fingers to play so fast.

_____   5. To even think of doing such things is sheer insanity.

_____   6. Don't be so bashful!

_____   7. The FBI exposed the scheme to defraud the government.

_____   8. Too many accolades from too many admirers went to his head.

_____   9. "Aha!" exclaimed the dentist. "A cavity!"

_____   10. I was so cold that I had absolutely no sensation in my hands or feet.

VOCABULARY   C. Word Meaning   6. *Can provide synonyms*

DIRECTIONS: For each underlined word under A, find the synonym under B and write the correct letter in the space provided.

A

_____ 1. They found the weather too rigorous.

_____ 2. Commerce between the two countries came to a standstill.

_____ 3. Mirror Lake is so called because it is almost always quiet.

_____ 4. For recreation, they threw horseshoes.

_____ 5. Bruno is not likely to forget the punishment he received.

_____ 6. Jane indicated her desire to withdraw from the contest.

_____ 7. Bob's van was furnished with electronic gear.

_____ 8. Although, his burden of sorrow was great, he stood tall and upright.

_____ 9. His anger spent, the speaker sat down exhausted.

_____ 10. Repeated injustices aroused the colonists to rebel.

B

a. serene
b. indignation
c. silence
d. equipped
e. escaped
f. still
g. climate
h. apt
i. erect
j. expressed
k. provoked
l. pitched
m. tossed
n. trade

VOCABULARY   C. Word Meaning   6. *Can provide synonyms*

DIRECTIONS: Circle the synonym of the first word on each line.

1.	transform	money	change	new	reform
2.	diminish	distance	menace	decrease	increase
3.	significant	signal	outstanding	important	large
4.	plan	scheme	fail	result	tear
5.	persevere	sweat	continue	pursue	cruel
6.	ingenious	engineer	native	talented	clever
7.	prohibit	forbid	protect	hide	condition
8.	obstinate	tenacious	proud	stubborn	haughty
9.	environment	park	atmosphere	forest	surroundings
10.	entertain	sing	amuse	dance	play

VOCABULARY   C. Word Meaning   *7. Can provide antonyms*

DIRECTIONS: Fill in the blanks with the antonym of each underlined word.

1. "The <u>rich</u> get richer and the _____ get poorer" is an often-heard statement.

2. "_____ and <u>Peace</u>" is the title of a novel by a famous Russian writer.

3. The piano teacher found the tempo too _____ for a selection that was written to be played <u>fast</u>.

4. Must we be subjected to _____ before we can truly appreciate <u>freedom</u>?

5. Giving _____ for achievement and for work well done, instead of <u>punishment</u> for work not done or poorly done, is a desirable form of discipline.

6. Many _____ homes cannot be moved at all because they have been made <u>stationary</u>.

7. The part of the evening when it is no longer daylight and not yet dark is called _____, while the reverse in the morning is called <u>dawn</u>.

8. If the <u>majority</u> is happy, that is likely to leave the _____ unhappy.

9. From <u>head</u> to _____, his outfit was elegant.

10. Swamps will not be found in <u>arid</u> _____ places.

VOCABULARY   C. Word Meaning   7. *Can provide antonyms*

DIRECTIONS: Match each word in column A with its antonym in column B. Write the letter of the antonym in the space provided.

	A		**B**
_____	1. vertical	a.	mild
		b.	grotesque
_____	2. ancient	c.	luxury
		d.	wrong
_____	3. sharp	e.	promote
		f.	horizontal
_____	4. hopeful	g.	unconscious
		h.	natural
_____	5. native	i.	desperate
		j.	sow
_____	6. poverty	k.	foreign
		l.	modern
_____	7. harvest	m.	sad
_____	8. right		
_____	9. frustrate		
_____	10. aware		

VOCABULARY   C. Word Meaning   7. *Can provide antonyms*

DIRECTIONS: For each underlined word in the sentences under A, find the antonym in column B and place its letter in the space provided. (The antonym will have nothing to do with the meaning of the sentence.)

A

_____ 1. <u>Distracted</u> students make a teacher's work difficult.

_____ 2. Many magicians' tricks are based on <u>illusion</u>.

_____ 3. The political parties <u>adopted</u> platforms.

_____ 4. Tulips and other early spring flowers <u>vanish</u> too fast.

_____ 5. The situation was awful and it was definitely not a <u>comedy</u>.

_____ 6. You should obey the <u>exit</u> sign strictly.

_____ 7. There were too many <u>participants</u> in the show.

_____ 8. "If <u>ignorance</u> is bliss, 'tis folly to be wise."

_____ 9. They exchanged <u>insults</u>.

_____ 10. When I knew him, he was still an <u>apprentice</u>.

B

a. abolished

b. swamp

c. tragedy

d. attentive

e. appear

f. insult

g. reality

h. compliments

i. entrance

j. master

k. spectators

l. learner

m. knowledge

n. civilian

VOCABULARY   C. Word Meaning   7. *Can provide antonyms*

DIRECTIONS: Circle the antonym of the first word in each line.

1.	civilian	parent	military	polite	cruel
2.	insufficient	lacking	rich	ample	suffering
3.	noisy	quiet	fast	loud	brash
4.	pleasure	feeling	liking	fit	anger
5.	lengthy	long	short	unending	abrupt
6.	sweet	odor	taste	bitter	pleasant
7.	receive	accept	give	obtain	secure
8.	abandon	redeem	leave	send	lift
9.	conceal	hide	speak	stamp	reveal
10.	descent	smell	odor	down	ascent

VOCABULARY   C. Word Meaning   8. *Understands homophones*

DIRECTIONS: From the list on the right, select the correct homophones for each sentence and write them in the proper spaces.

1. The pirates on the high _____ tried

    to _____ the ship that was carrying gold.

2. Last year, _____ student from our school

    lost; another _____.

3. The _____ of Helen's skunk _____

    everyone running indoors.

4. Trucks have to stop at _____ stations on

    their _____ from one state to another.

5. The sun _____ hot and bright upon the

    tourists who were being _____ the view.

   seas

   one

   scent

   weigh

   shone

   way

   sent

   seize

   won

   shown

6. The _____ of the egg spotted the

    _____ of her dress.

7. With all that noise, you can't _____

    me even when I'm standing right _____ .

8. As they caught _____ of their home

    on the old familiar _____, they cried.

9. "Haven't you _____?" the cowboy yelled.

    "The _____ is stampeding!"

10. Mother liked to listen to _____ singing

    her favorite _____ .

   hear

   yolk

   hymn

   site

   herd

   yoke

   heard

   here

   him

   sight

VOCABULARY   C. Word Meaning   *8. Understands homophones*

DIRECTIONS: In each of the sentences below, cross out the homophone that does not make sense for that sentence.

1. One <u>bale   bail   </u> of cotton was piled on top of another.

2. To attend the movie would be a sheer <u>waist   waste   </u> of time.

3. Acre after acre was used to grow sugar <u>beats   beets   </u> .

4. Every girl dreams of being the <u>bell   belle   </u> of the ball.

5. The boys have gone hunting with their sisters; the <u>deer   dear   </u> season just opened.

6. Doctor Mac had difficulty finding a <u>vane   vein   </u> big enough for the injection.

7. Do not do anything that <u>yule   you'll   </u> later regret.

8. I must get my dog a collar; he has <u>flees   fleas   </u> .

9. When he tried to throw the basketball, he stepped over the <u>foul   fowl   </u> line.

10. We had a <u>fur   fir   </u> tree for Christmas.

VOCABULARY   C. Word Meaning   8. *Understands homophones*

DIRECTIONS: Write the homophones for each definition.

1. It covers your head.   a. _____

    It had a race with the tortoise.   b. _____

2. You look this way when you are afraid.   c. _____

    Another word for bucket.   d. _____

3. You appear this way if you do not wear clothes. e. _____

    A large, furry animal that sleeps all winter.   f. _____

4. What you do when you employ someone.   g. _____

    The way you would want your kite to fly.   h. _____

5. Inactive, doing nothing.   i. _____

    An object of blind devotion.   j. _____

6. Gravel feels this way, but sand does not.   k. _____

    It is best to let things take their _____ .   l. _____

7. It is worn on the finger.   m. _____

    When you twist with force.   n. _____

8. The color that means danger.   o. _____

    You're doing it now and you probably did it   p. _____
    yesterday.

9. You get bargains here.   q. _____

    The wind propels a boat with one.   r. _____

10. Two or three; not many.   s. _____

    You say this before you say, "It's hot!"   t. _____

VOCABULARY   C. Word Meaning   8. *Understands homophones*

DIRECTIONS: Write the correct homophone to complete each sentence.

1. Put the golf ball on the _____.   a. _____

   A favorite iced drink is _____.   b. _____

2. Admiral Byrd went to the South _____.   c. _____

   To see how people felt about it, they took a _____.   d. _____

3. To make bread, the baker kneads _____.   e. _____

   The musician begins his scale with _____.   f. _____

4. The prospectors took all of the ore from the _____.   g. _____

   Poor donkey; it refused to pull the _____.   h. _____

5. Before Christmas, you want to take a _____.   i. _____

   Have you ever climbed to the top of Pike's _____?   j. _____

6. What clothes will you _____?   k. _____

   _____ will you go?   l. _____

7. When he met us, all he said was _____.   m. _____

   Everyone agreed that the price was too _____.   n. _____

8. While sitting at the piano, I struck a _____.   o. _____

   Father cut a _____ of wood.   p. _____

9. The bride's father led her to the _____.   q. _____

   We will not _____ the rule for quiet.   r. _____

10. A green and sweet melon is called a honey _____.   s. _____

    The suitor said, "Marry me, Honey, please _____.   t. _____

VOCABULARY   C. Word Meaning   9. *Understands homographs*

DIRECTIONS: In the blanks, write homographs from the definitions given.

1. The speech was a _____. It _____ no resemblance to
    (tiresome)   (past tense of "bear")
    what had been announced.

2. Please _____ the window. It is _____ to my desk.
    (shut)   (near)

3. The _____ of Miss Bea's eyes dilated. She had shut off the lights to
    (part of the eye)
    show her _____ a filmstrip.
    (students)

4. If the Boy Scouts _____ all the newspapers they collected, they will
    (tie and wrap together)
    make a _____ .
    (a lot of money)

5. Some states do not _____ a young person to get a driving
    (allow)
    _____ until he or she is sixteen.
    (written license)

6. She refuses to wear the color _____ . She says it makes her feel
    (color of sky)
    _____ .
    (unhappy)

7. The First National _____ is located on the _____ of
    (where money is kept)   (shore, slope)
    the New River.

8. Running after the _____ , the milkmaid stumbled and hurt the
    (baby cow)
    _____ of her leg.
    (lower part of her leg)

VOCABULARY   C. Word Meaning   *9. Understands homographs*

DIRECTIONS: For each underlined word in the following sentences, three meanings are given. Fill in the circle in front of the meaning that best expresses the idea of the word as it is used in the sentence.

1. Inspectors found that one cable of the suspension bridge was weak.
   o a. to send a message
   o b. strong rope or chain
   o c. overseas message

2. The Community Chest was conducting a campaign for funds.
   o a. upper part of the body
   o b. a strong box
   o c. treasury of a charitable institution

3. A kind of crab is named after the state of Maryland where it is found.
   o a. shellfish
   o b. sour person
   o c. to complain

4. Good cooks will tell you to add a dash of this and a pinch of that.
   o a. a short race
   o b. hurry off
   o c. a little bit

5. Be sure to fix supper so it will be ready when everybody is home.
   o a. fasten
   o b. prepare
   o c. repair

6. Hold this while I stretch it tight.
   o a. inside of a ship
   o b. to keep possession
   o c. grasp

7. On the Fourth of July, the family went to the County Fair.
   o a. without cheating
   o b. a show or exhibition
   o c. not cloudy

8. Elvis Presley had countless fans.
   o a. objects that move air
   o b. great admirers
   o c. makes a breeze

9. Betty bought a head of cabbage.
   o a. the top part
   o b. take a certain direction
   o c. chief person

10. To trust someone is to have complete faith in that person.
   o a. a religion
   o b. confidence
   o c. belief without proof

VOCABULARY   C. Word Meaning   9. *Understands homographs*

DIRECTIONS: Write the homograph for each set of definitions below.

1.   a busy sound
      to sing with closed lips   _____

2.   not plain
      to imagine   _____

3.   to go down or under
      a place for washing dishes   _____

4.   a disreputable place
      to jump into water head first   _____

5.   to signal
      a cloth emblem of a nation   _____

6.   animal skin
      to put out of sight   _____

7.   a weapon
      to step on the gas   _____

8.   a row that has been plowed
      to wrinkle   _____

9.   a kind of fish
      a bird's resting place   _____

10.   favorite
      to stroke   _____

VOCABULARY   C. Word Meaning   9. *Understands homographs*

DIRECTIONS: Write the homograph for each set of meanings given.

1.   25 cents
      1/4   _____

2.   a contest
      a kind of people   _____

3.   not cooked
      cold and damp   _____

4.   a free ticket
      a way through the mountains   _____

5.   something to cook in
      to strain out gold   _____

6.   a bundle
      to fill tightly   _____

7.   to pass the tongue over
      to whip   _____

8.   a written message
      an athlete's award   _____

9.   to cover with metal
      home base   _____

10.   a tool to press clothes
      a tool to brand cattle   _____

VOCABULARY   C. Word Meaning   10. *Can write metaphors*
                                 11. *Can write similes*

DIRECTIONS: Carefully read the following sentences. Distinguish whether each one contains a metaphor or a simile and write <u>metaphor</u> or <u>simile</u> in the space provided. If the sentence has neither, write <u>none</u>.

1. The sword will glut itself with blood.   _____

2. Disloyalty is like a disease.   _____

3. Sad but courageous, she wandered
   through the desert of her life.   _____

4. The crippled ship went down like lead.   _____

5. Cruel words are arrows that cause pain.   _____

6. Like dolls, the performers danced stiffly.   _____

7. Bees buzzed their way to the perfumed
   breath of the apple blossoms.   _____

8. A red veil of little buds signaled the tree's
   shy awakening.   _____

9. The leaves of the sumac burning red and
   gold gloriously confirmed that autumn
   was at hand.   _____

10. After midnight, city streets are silent
    canyons.   _____

VOCABULARY   C. Word Meaning   10. *Can write metaphors*
                                   11. *Can write similes*

DIRECTIONS: Carefully read the following sentences. Distinguish whether each one contains a metaphor or a simile and write metaphor or simile in the space provided. If the sentence has neither, write none.

1. Her laughter cheered us like a happy tune. _____

2. In the springtime of his life, he wondered what he would have accomplished when his winter came. _____

3. Fears are phantoms of the imagination. _____

4. Stripped by winter stood the skeleton trees. _____

5. Her comings were always like hurricanes, sudden and devastating. _____

6. His anger was unleashed, and he poured it on them like a flood. _____

7. A laughing spell is good medicine. _____

8. The moon was a spotlight for the leafy branches dancing on the bedroom wall. _____

9. Violence, like a tornado, destroys everything in its path. _____

10. Even in his early youth, he was as strong as an ox. _____

VOCABULARY   C. Word Meaning   10. *Can write metaphors*
                                 11. *Can write similes*

DIRECTIONS: In a metaphor, two things are said to be alike by giving one the characteristics of the other or by making one act like the other. Keeping this in mind, see if you can write at least five metaphors with the ideas suggested by the words, pairs of words, or phrases given below. Be creative! Be fanciful!

*** shadows   *** sunset   *** snow—magic
*** a person—a cyclone   *** lights—a bridge—night   *** old age

1. _____

2. _____

3. _____

4. _____

5. _____

DIRECTIONS: Listed below are words and phrases that could give you ideas for writing similes. Using them in any way you like, at the beginning, in the middle, or at the end of your simile, write at least five similes. Remember that the words <u>as</u> or <u>like</u> are necessary in a simile. If none of the suggestions inspire you, make up some of your own.

*** like a madman ...   *** brave as ...   *** feeling loved is like ...
*** like foam upon the water ... *** ... as thorns   *** stubborn as .. .

1. _____

2. _____

3. _____

4. _____

5. _____

VOCABULARY   C. Word Meaning   10. *Can write metaphors*
                                 11. *Can write similes*

DIRECTIONS: Write at least five metaphors. Use the ideas suggested by the words, pairs of words, or phrases listed below. Be creative! Be fanciful! Be different! The words need not be exactly those listed, but something they awaken in your mind.

*** joy—a garment   *** thoughts—a swarm of   *** strength
*** a field of wheat, corn,   bees   *** darkness—a mine
    or daisies   *** the action of the surf

1. _____

2. _____

3. _____

4. _____

5. _____

DIRECTIONS: Listed below are words and phrases that could give you ideas for writing similes. Use them in any way you wish. See if you can write at least five similes. Come up with some new ideas!

*** like rust that corrodes   *** dry as ...   *** fragile as ...
*** ... as gold   *** giggling like ... *** like the morning dew

1. _____

2. _____

3. _____

4. _____

5. _____

WORD ATTACK   **A. Phonic and Structural Characteristics of Words**
                      1. *Knows initial consonants and blends*

DIRECTIONS: Read the words below. Underline the initial consonant or consonant blend that begins each word. On the line, write *c* for initial consonant or *bl* for consonant blend. Leave the space blank if the word begins with a vowel.

1. scold	_____	11. start	_____
2. bread	_____	12. creepy	_____
3. shirt	_____	13. usual	_____
4. easily	_____	14. intricate	_____
5. keep	_____	15. wild	_____
6. genteel	_____	16. zipper	_____
7. draft	_____	17. turnkey	_____
8. lesson	_____	18. tote	_____
9. eyes	_____	19. shop	_____
10. few	_____	20. escort	_____

WORD ATTACK   A. Phonic and Structural Characteristics of Words
              1. *Knows initial consonants and blends*

DIRECTIONS: Read the words below. Underline the initial consonant or consonant blend that begins each word. On the line, write *c* for initial consonant or *bl* for consonant blend. Leave the space blank if the word begins with a vowel.

1. first	_____	11. and	_____
2. even	_____	12. flush	_____
3. plentiful	_____	13. inherit	_____
4. care	_____	14. wharf	_____
5. clean	_____	15. zap	_____
6. open	_____	16. thirty	_____
7. crack	_____	17. write	_____
8. delicate	_____	18. fever	_____
9. float	_____	19. syrup	_____
10. nice	_____	20. treat	_____

WORD ATTACK   **A. Phonic and Structural Characteristics of Words**
              1. *Knows initial consonants and blends*

DIRECTIONS: Read the words below. Underline the initial consonant or consonant blend that begins each word. On the line, write *c* for initial consonant or *bl* for consonant blend. Leave the space blank if the word begins with a vowel.

1. poor	_____	11. jump	_____
2. laugh	_____	12. iron	_____
3. write	_____	13. voice	_____
4. cooked	_____	14. zero	_____
5. shape	_____	15. truck	_____
6. finger	_____	16. present	_____
7. escort	_____	17. droop	_____
8. mouth	_____	18. uncle	_____
9. plate	_____	19. twinkle	_____
10. twist	_____	20. rich	_____

WORD ATTACK   A. Phonic and Structural Characteristics of Words
1. *Knows initial consonants and blends*

DIRECTIONS: Read the words below. Underline the initial consonant or consonant blend that begins each word. On the line, write *c* for initial consonant or *bl* for consonant blend. Leave the space blank if the word begins with a vowel.

1. breakfast	_____	11. ice	_____
2. ale	_____	12. hold	_____
3. great	_____	13. wrong	_____
4. teach	_____	14. tiny	_____
5. nothing	_____	15. plot	_____
6. elegant	_____	16. dwelling	_____
7. slug	_____	17. upon	_____
8. ask	_____	18. twist	_____
9. pride	_____	19. shake	_____
10. gloat	_____	20. ruffle	_____

WORD ATTACK   **A. Phonic and Structural Characteristics of Words**
    2. *Knows short and long vowels*

DIRECTIONS: Write the vowel and the correct diacritical mark on the line next to each word.

$$\bar{a}, \breve{a}, \bar{e}, \breve{e}, \bar{i}, \breve{i}, \bar{o}, \breve{o}, \bar{u}, \breve{u}$$

1. base   _____

2. cheap   _____

3. cope   _____

4. fall   _____

5. felt   _____

6. hit   _____

7. pop   _____

8. cod   _____

9. hug   _____

10. fight   _____

WORD ATTACK   A. Phonic and Structural Characteristics of Words
   2. Knows short and long vowels

DIRECTIONS: Write the vowel and the correct diacritical mark on the line next to each word.

$$\bar{a}, \ \breve{a}, \ \bar{e}, \ \breve{e}, \ \bar{i}, \ \breve{i}, \ \bar{o}, \ \breve{o}, \ \bar{u}, \ \breve{u}$$

1. he   _____

2. bing   _____

3. dance   _____

4. fret   _____

5. kite   _____

6. mug   _____

7. fat   _____

8. hope   _____

9. mete   _____

10. cop   _____

WORD ATTACK   A. Phonic and Structural Characteristics of Words
              2. *Knows short and long vowels*

DIRECTIONS: Write the vowel and the correct diacritical mark on the line next to each word.

$\bar{a}$, $\breve{a}$, $\bar{e}$, $\breve{e}$, $\bar{i}$, $\breve{i}$, $\bar{o}$, $\breve{o}$, $\bar{u}$, $\breve{u}$

1. it   _____

2. carry   _____

3. shop   _____

4. feet   _____

5. ugly   _____

6. blow   _____

7. time   _____

8. bet   _____

9. hall   _____

10. might   _____

Name: _____ Date: _____

WORD ATTACK   A. Phonic and Structural Characteristics of Words
               2. *Knows short and long vowels*

DIRECTIONS: Write the vowel and the correct diacritical mark on the line next to each word.

$\bar{a}$, $\breve{a}$, $\bar{e}$, $\breve{e}$, $\bar{i}$, $\breve{i}$, $\bar{o}$, $\breve{o}$, $\bar{u}$, $\breve{u}$

1. apple   _____

2. slow   _____

3. sing   _____

4. seep   _____

5. fire   _____

6. night   _____

7. kept   _____

8. pate   _____

9. sop   _____

10. shut   _____

WORD ATTACK   **B. Vowel Sounds**   **1. *Knows vowel rules***
                                        a. When there is only one vowel in a
                                             word or syllable, the vowel is short

DIRECTIONS: On the line next to each word listed below, rewrite the word, putting in the correct diacritical or vowel sound mark.

1. end   _____

2. just   _____

3. low   _____

4. curl   _____

5. six   _____

6. high   _____

7. when   _____

8. drunk   _____

9. land   _____

10. she   _____

Name: _____ Date: _____

WORD ATTACK   **B. Vowel Sounds**   **1. *Knows vowel rules***
                                           a. When there is only one vowel in a
                                           word or syllable, the vowel is short

DIRECTIONS: On the line next to each word listed below, rewrite the word, putting in the correct diacritical or vowel sound mark.

   1. toe   _____

   2. stamp   _____

   3. him   _____

   4. novel   _____

   5. arid   _____

   6. ale   _____

   7. puck   _____

   8. power   _____

   9. bust   _____

 10. dell   _____

WORD ATTACK **B. Vowel Sounds** **1. *Knows vowel rules***
a. When there is only one vowel in a
word or syllable, the vowel is short

DIRECTIONS: Read the word at the beginning of each line. Circle the word on the same line that has the correct vowel sound symbol.

	A	*B*
1. man	măn	mān
2. clock	clōck	clŏck
3. get	gĕt	gēt
4. cop	cōp	cŏp
5. struck	strūck	strŭck
6. case	cāse	căse
7. no	nō	nŏ
8. cup	cūp	cŭp
9. feel	fēel	fĕel
10. dust	dūst	dŭst

Name: _____ Date: _____

WORD ATTACK   **B. Vowel Sounds**   1. *Knows vowel rules*
         a. When there is only one vowel in a
          word or syllable, the vowel is short

DIRECTIONS: Read the word at the beginning of each line. Circle the word on the same line that has the correct vowel sound symbol.

	A	*B*
1. prick	prīck	prĭck
2. belt	bĕlt	bēlt
3. pen	pēn	pĕn
4. bump	bŭmp	būmp
5. settle	sēttle	sĕttle
6. bad	băd	bād
7. ride	rĭde	rīde
8. rid	rĭd	rīd
9. inn	īnn	ĭnn
10. mum	mūm	mŭm

WORD ATTACK   **B. Vowel Sounds**   1. *Knows vowel rules*
b. When there are two vowels in a word or syllable, the first vowel is long and the second is silent

---

DIRECTIONS: The word in the first column below is repeated three times, with different diacritical marks and slashes to indicate silent vowels. Find and circle the correct one for each.

		A	*B*	*C*
1.	fine	fīne	fīnē	finȩ́
2.	haze	hăzȩ́	hāzȩ́	hăzĕ
3.	tie	tīȩ́	tīe	tȩ́ē
4.	peat	pȩ́āt	pēȩ́t	pēat
5.	shoddy	shŏddȳ̸	shŏddȳ	shŏddȳ̸
6.	file	fīlȩ́	fĭlȩ́	fĭle
7.	haste	hāstĕ	hāstȩ́	hăstȩ́
8.	pale	pālȩ́	pălĕ	pālȩ́
9.	these	thȩ́sē	thēsȩ́	thĕsĕ
10.	lime	lȋmĕ	līmĕ	līmȩ́

WORD ATTACK   B. Vowel Sounds   1. *Knows vowel rules*
   b. When there are two vowels in a word or syllable, the first vowel is long and the second is silent

---

DIRECTIONS: The word in the first column below is repeated three times, with different diacritical marks and slashes to indicate silent vowels. Find and circle the correct one for each.

		A	B	C
1.	hale	hāle	hāl√	hăle
2.	life	lĭfe	līfe	līf√
3.	clove	clōv√	clōve	clŏv√
4.	taste	tāste	tăste	tāst√
5.	ache	āche	ăch√	āch√
6.	pal	pāl	păl	p√l
7.	strange	străng√	strānge	străng√
8.	face	făc√	fāc√	fāce
9.	side	sĭd√	sīde	sīd√
10.	froze	frōz√	frōze	frŏz√

WORD ATTACK   **B. Vowel Sounds**   **1.** *Knows vowel rules*
b. When there are two vowels in a word or syllable, the first vowel is long and the second is silent

DIRECTIONS: Read each of the following words carefully. Then, place a breve (‿) over the short vowel sound, a macron (—) over the long vowel sound, and a slash (/) through the silent letter.

1. those

2. opal

3. fop

4. lad

5. while

6. smile

7. made

8. road

9. wreathed

10. flake

WORD ATTACK   B. Vowel Sounds   1. *Knows vowel rules*
                                    b. When there are two vowels in a word
                                       or syllable, the first vowel is long and
                                       the second is silent

DIRECTIONS: Read each of the following words carefully. Then, place a breve (˘) over the short vowel sound, a macron (—) over the long vowel sound, and a slash (/) through the silent letter.

1. clean

2. name

3. mole

4. stale

5. waste

6. stole

7. knife

8. ride

9. whit

10. white

WORD ATTACK   **B. Vowel Sounds**   **1. *Knows vowel rules***
   c. When there are two vowels together, the first is long and the second is silent

DIRECTIONS: The words in the first column below are repeated twice, with different vowel markings and silent vowels omitted. Find and circle the correct one for each.

		A	*B*
1.	clean	klĕn	klēn
2.	straight	străt	strāt
3.	flue	flo͞o	flŭ
4.	tie	tī	tĭ
5.	boast	bŏst	bōst
6.	see	sē	sĕ
7.	feast	fĕst	fēst
8.	free	frē	frĕ
9.	fret	frĕt	frēt
10.	raise	răz	rāz

WORD ATTACK   **B. Vowel Sounds**   1. *Knows vowel rules*
c. When there are two vowels together, the first is long and the second is silent

DIRECTIONS: Read each of the following words carefully. Then, place a breve (˘) over the short vowel sound, a macron (—) over the long vowel sound, and a slash (/) through the silent vowel.

1. peace

2. pail

3. vie

4. boat

5. sheep

6. afraid

7. treat

8. toe

9. glue

10. beaver

WORD ATTACK   B. Vowel Sounds   **1. *Knows vowel rules***
c. When there are two vowels together, the first is long and the second is silent

DIRECTIONS: The words in the first column below are repeated twice, with different vowel markings and silent vowels omitted. Find and circle the correct one for each.

		A	*B*
1.	cue	kyo͞o	kyo͝o
2.	lie	lī	lĭ
3.	gloat	glŏt	glōt
4.	chain	chān	chăn
5.	feet	fĕt	fēt
6.	seat	sēt	sĕt
7.	need	nĕd	nēd
8.	unload	ŭnlōd	ŭnlŏd
9.	pain	păn	pān
10.	each	ĕch	ēch

WORD ATTACK   **B. Vowel Sounds**   **1. *Knows vowel rules***
c. When there are two vowels together, the first is long and the second is silent

DIRECTIONS: Each word is written twice, once as you usually see it and the second time with vowel symbols. On the line next to the words, write *yes* if the vowel markings are correct and *no* if the markings are incorrect.

1. steal	stēl	_____
2. due	do͞o	_____
3. oath	ŏth	_____
4. cheat	chĕt	_____
5. really	rēlē	_____
6. pie	pī	_____
7. keep	kĕp	_____
8. neat	nēt	_____
9. goes	gōz	_____
10. sneak	snēk	_____

WORD ATTACK   C. Syllabication   1. *Knows rules for syllables*
a. Each syllable must have a vowel and a single vowel can be a syllable

DIRECTIONS: Read the following words. Write the number of syllables in each word on the line next to the word.

1. yourself	_____	11. letter	_____
2. lifted	_____	12. vulture	_____
3. tendency	_____	13. translate	_____
4. stadium	_____	14. presence	_____
5. register	_____	15. pantry	_____
6. official	_____	16. impressive	_____
7. justify	_____	17. genuine	_____
8. momentum	_____	18. formula	_____
9. exhaust	_____	19. intention	_____
10. ditch	_____	20. hazardous	_____

WORD ATTACK   C. Syllabication   1. *Knows rules for syllables*
                  a. Each syllable must have a vowel and a
                  single vowel can be a syllable

DIRECTIONS: Read the following words. Write the number of syllables in each word on the line next to the word.

1. following	_____		11. pronunciation	_____
2. however	_____		12. wardrobe	_____
3. tender	_____		13. transfer	_____
4. spherical	_____		14. panic	_____
5. ordinance	_____		15. recover	_____
6. humble	_____		16. pressure	_____
7. merchandise	_____		17. fleet	_____
8. expedition	_____		18. inherit	_____
9. coastal	_____		19. generosity	_____
10. cove	_____		20. division	_____

WORD ATTACK   **C. Syllabication**   **1. *Knows rules for syllables***
          a. Each syllable must have a vowel and a single vowel can be a syllable

DIRECTIONS: Read each of the following words to yourself. Write the number of syllables in each word on the line next to the word.

1. vowel	_____	11. sentences	_____
2. whinny	_____	12. touching	_____
3. symbol	_____	13. skeptical	_____
4. suspicious	_____	14. pitch	_____
5. pinto	_____	15. ridicule	_____
6. monitor	_____	16. pursue	_____
7. murmur	_____	17. irrigate	_____
8. dignity	_____	18. horizontal	_____
9. delegate	_____	19. marsh	_____
10. frequent	_____	20. exterior	_____

WORD ATTACK   C. Syllabication   1. *Knows rules for syllables*
a. Each syllable must have a vowel and a single vowel can be a syllable

DIRECTIONS: Read each of the following words to yourself. Write the number of syllables in each word on the line next to the word.

1. number	_____		11. beautiful	_____
2. passing	_____		12. unfurl	_____
3. tantrum	_____		13. spider	_____
4. supporter	_____		14. pinwheel	_____
5. reluctant	_____		15. musket	_____
6. pine	_____		16. indigestion	_____
7. mournful	_____		17. frantic	_____
8. engrave	_____		18. granite	_____
9. jeer	_____		19. desperate	_____
10. coyote	_____		20. mascot	_____

WORD ATTACK   C. Syllabication   1. *Knows rules for syllables*
                                        b. The root is a syllable and is not divided

DIRECTIONS: Circle the word in column A or column B that gives the correct syllabication of each word.

		A	B
1.	slowly	slow ly	slo wly
2.	alone	al one	a lone
3.	charger	charg er	char ger
4.	inside	ins ide	in side
5.	exact	ex act	e xact
6.	judgment	judg ment	judgm ent
7.	sureness	sure ness	suren ess
8.	grassy	gras sy	grass y
9.	hateful	hatef ul	hate ful
10.	warning	war ning	warn ing

WORD ATTACK   C. Syllabication   1. *Knows rules for syllables*
                                   b. The root is a syllable and is not
                                      divided

DIRECTIONS: Circle the word in column A or column B that gives the correct syllabication of each word.

		A	*B*
1.	welcome	welc ome	wel come
2.	woeful	woe ful	woef ul
3.	mistake	mis take	mist ake
4.	intent	int ent	in tent
5.	drinking	drin king	drink ing
6.	almost	alm ost	al most
7.	dusty	dust y	dus ty
8.	extend	ext end	ex tend
9.	behold	be hold	beh old
10.	shapeless	sha peless	shape less

WORD ATTACK   C. Syllabication   1. *Knows rules for syllables*
                                        b. The root is a syllable and is not
                                              divided

DIRECTIONS: Divide each of the words listed below into syllables. Circle the part of the word that is the root.

1. standard   _____

2. hitter   _____

3. fishy   _____

4. disuse   _____

5. training   _____

6. staffer   _____

7. unfailing   _____

8. killer   _____

9. sublet   _____

10. trident   _____

WORD ATTACK **C. Syllabication** **1.** *Knows rules for syllables*
b. The root is a syllable and is not divided

DIRECTIONS: Divide each of the words listed below into syllables. Circle the part of the word which is the root.

1. waiting _____

2. resolve _____

3. plainly _____

4. forehead _____

5. disarm _____

6. approve _____

7. around _____

8. helpless _____

9. disclose _____

10. boastful _____

WORD ATTACK   C. Syllabication   1. *Knows rules for syllables*
                                       c. Blends are not divided

DIRECTIONS: For each word listed below:
1. Under column A, circle the blend or blends.
2. Under column B, on the blank, write the letter that is at the top of the column in which
   you find the correct division of the word into syllables.

A	B			
	ⓐ	ⓑ	ⓒ	
1. tripod	t ri pod	trip od	tri pod	_____
2. shyness	s hy ness	shy ness	sh y ness	_____
3. crawl	c raw l	cr awl	crawl	_____
4. greatly	great ly	g reat ly	gr eatl y	_____
5. dread	dr ead	d read	dread	_____
6. floodgate	f lood gate	flood gate	fl ood gate	_____
7. smart	s mart	sm art	smart	_____
8. driven	driv en	d riv en	dri ven	_____
9. slipshod	s lips hod	slip shod	sl ips hod	_____
10. price	price	p rice	pr ice	_____

WORD ATTACK   C. Syllabication   1. *Knows rules for syllables*
                                  c. Blends are not divided

DIRECTIONS: For each word listed below:
1. Under column A, circle the blend or blends.
2. Under column B, on the blank, write the letter that is at the top of the column in which
   you find the correct division of the word into syllables.

	A		B		
		ⓐ	ⓑ	ⓒ	
1.	sparrow	sp ar row	spar row	s parr ow	_____
2.	frankly	fr ank ly	frank ly	fran kly	_____
3.	flush	f lush	fl u sh	flush	_____
4.	craven	cra ven	crav en	cr a ven	_____
5.	promise	prom ise	p rom ise	pro mise	_____
6.	friend	fri end	friend	fr iend	_____
7.	drowning	d rown ing	drown ing	dr own ing	_____
8.	gluey	g lu ey	gl u ey	glu ey	_____
9.	plasma	p las ma	plas ma	pl as ma	_____
10.	snowing	snow ing	s now ing	sno wing	_____

WORD ATTACK   **C. Syllabication**   **1.** *Knows rules for syllables*
         c. Blends are not divided

DIRECTIONS: From each line, select the form of the word that is correctly divided into syllables. Then, write the correct form in the space to the right.

1. d ry ness   dr y ness   dry ness   _____

2. fl op py   flop py   f lop py   _____

3. ghos tli ke   ghost like   gh ost like   _____

4. p ride ful   pri de ful   pride ful   _____

5. s ky lark   sky lark   sk yl ark   _____

6. tri umph   tr iump h   tri um ph   _____

7. tri ad   tr i ad   t ri ad   _____

8. spouse   s pou se   sp ouse   _____

9. gl o ry   g lor y   glo ry   _____

10. c row ded   crowd ed   cr owd ed   _____

WORD ATTACK   C. Syllabication   1. *Knows rules for syllables*
c. Blends are not divided

DIRECTIONS: Read each of the following words carefully. Then, on the blank line, write the word divided into syllables.

1. creepy   _____

2. slowness   _____

3. drought   _____

4. skier   _____

5. flaming   _____

6. bloated   _____

7. grandee   _____

8. plush   _____

9. tryout   _____

10. chalk   _____

WORD ATTACK   **C. Syllabication**   **1. *Knows rules for syllables***
                                            d. Suffixes and prefixes are syllables

DIRECTIONS: Underline the prefixes in the words listed below and circle the suffixes. Then, on the line provided, write the word, dividing it into syllables.

1. inspect   _____

2. boyhood   _____

3. actor   _____

4. peaceful   _____

5. exile   _____

6. upend   _____

7. seamless   _____

8. submerge   _____

9. reduce   _____

10. wholesome   _____

Name: _____ Date: _____

DIRECTIONS: Divide each of the following words as if it were at the end of a line.

1. misprint   _____

2. guileless   _____

3. emerge   _____

4. graceful   _____

5. childhood   _____

6. semicircle   _____

7. review   _____

8. oily   _____

9. doer   _____

10. extend   _____

WORD ATTACK   C. Syllabication   1. *Knows rules for syllables*
                                              d. Suffixes and prefixes are syllables

DIRECTIONS: Look carefully at the words listed below and say them to yourself. Write each word, dividing it into syllables. Underline prefixes and circle suffixes.

1. dancer   _____

2. export   _____

3. humidity   _____

4. intone   _____

5. wayward   _____

6. preview   _____

7. gutless   _____

8. powerful   _____

9. falsehood   _____

10. circumscribe   _____

Name: _____ Date: _____

WORD ATTACK   C. Syllabication   1. *Knows rules for syllables*
                                   d. Suffixes and prefixes are syllables

DIRECTIONS: Look carefully at the words listed below. Write each word, dividing it into syllables. Underline prefixes and circle suffixes.

1. adjust   _____

2. jester   _____

3. bisect   _____

4. revive   _____

5. thankful   _____

6. girlhood   _____

7. humanly   _____

8. sleeveless   _____

9. toward   _____

10. exhaust   _____

WORD ATTACK   C. Syllabication   1. *Knows rules for syllables*
              e. Suffix *-ed* if preceded by a single *d* or *t*
              usually forms a separate syllable

DIRECTIONS: Circle, under column A or column B, the correct syllabication for each word in the column on the left.

		A	*B*
1.	requested	re ques ted	re quest ed
2.	crowded	crowd ed	crow ded
3.	doubted	doub ted	doubt ed
4.	regarded	re gar ded	re gard ed
5.	besotted	be sot ted	be sott ed
6.	responded	re spond ed	re spon ded
7.	kidded	kidd ed	kid ded
8.	invited	in vit ed	in vi ted
9.	ended	end ed	en ded
10.	suspended	sus pend ed	sus pen ded

WORD ATTACK   C. Syllabication   1. *Knows rules for syllables*

    e. Suffix *-ed* if preceded by a single *d* or *t* usually forms a separate syllable

DIRECTIONS: Circle, under column A or column B, the correct syllabication for each word in the column on the left.

	A	*B*
1. budded	bud ded	budd ed
2. preceded	pre ced ed	pre ce ded
3. resorted	re sor ted	re sort ed
4. clouded	clou ded	cloud ed
5. needed	need ed	nee ded
6. branded	bran ded	brand ed
7. faded	fad ed	fa ded
8. plotted	plott ed	plot ted
9. sanded	sand ed	san ded
10. padded	padd ed	pad ded

WORD ATTACK   C. Syllabication   **1.** *Knows rules for syllables*
   e. Suffix *-ed* if preceded by a single *d* or *t*
   usually forms a separate syllable

DIRECTIONS: Keeping in mind the rule stated above, syllabicate the following words.

1. trotted   _____

2. studded   _____

3. granted   _____

4. reflected   _____

5. wanted   _____

6. kneaded   _____

7. expected   _____

8. contented   _____

9. deeded   _____

10. rested   _____

WORD ATTACK   C. Syllabication   1. *Knows rules for syllables*
    e. Suffix *-ed* if preceded by a single *d* or *t*
       usually forms a separate syllable

DIRECTIONS: Say each of the following words to yourself. Circle the correct syllabication of each word in column A or column B.

		A	B
1.	heated	hea ted	heat ed
2.	heeded	heed ed	hee ded
3.	petted	pett ed	pet ted
4.	sledded	sledd ed	sled ded
5.	goaded	goad ed	goa ded
6.	nodded	nod ded	nodd ed
7.	pleaded	plead ed	plea ded
8.	sorted	sor ted	sort ed
9.	hosted	host ed	hos ted
10.	prodded	prod ded	prodd ed

WORD ATTACK   C. Syllabication   1. *Knows rules for syllables*
f. If a vowel in a syllable is followed by two consonants, the syllable ends with the first consonant

DIRECTIONS: Circle the correct syllabication for each word below.

	A	*B*	*C*
1. render	rend er	re nd er	ren der
2. written	wr it ten	writ ten	writt en
3. courteous	cour te ous	cour teous	court eous
4. struggle	strug gle	st rug gle	strugg le
5. purpose	purp ose	pur pose	pur po se
6. rumple	rump le	ru mp le	rum ple
7. diction	di ct ion	dic tion	dict ion
8. content	con ten t	con tent	cont ent
9. running	runn ing	run ni ng	run ning
10. wonder	wo nd er	wond er	won der

WORD ATTACK   C. Syllabication   **1. *Knows rules for syllables***
                  f. If a vowel in a syllable is followed by
                  two consonants, the syllable ends with
                  the first consonant

DIRECTIONS: Circle the correct syllabication for each word below.

	A	*B*	*C*
1. further	fur ther	furth er	furt her
2. mercy	merc y	mer cy	me r cy
3. concert	co nc ert	conc ert	con cert
4. argue	arg ue	argu e	ar gue
5. allow	all ow	al low	a ll ow
6. formula	form u la	form ul a	for mu la
7. common	comm on	co mm on	com mon
8. problem	prob lem	pro blem	probl em
9. actual	act u al	ac tu al	a ct u al
10. public	pu blic	pub lic	publ ic

WORD ATTACK   C. Syllabication   1. *Knows rules for syllables*
    f. If a vowel in a syllable is followed by
    two consonants, the syllable ends with
    the first consonant

DIRECTIONS: Rewrite each of the following words divided into syllables.

1. urgent   _____

2. blurring   _____

3. pristine   _____

4. collective   _____

5. action   _____

6. entire   _____

7. certain   _____

8. lesson   _____

9. party   _____

10. person   _____

WORD ATTACK   C. Syllabication   **1. *Knows rules for syllables***
f. If a vowel in a syllable is followed by two consonants, the syllable ends with the first consonant

DIRECTIONS: Read each word to yourself. Then, fill in the circle in front of the correct syllabication.

1. portage
   - ○ a.   port age
   - ○ b.   por tage
   - ○ c.   po rt age
   - ○ d.   portage

2. justice
   - ○ a.   ju stice
   - ○ b.   just ice
   - ○ c.   justi ce
   - ○ d.   jus tice

3. question
   - ○ a.   ques tion
   - ○ b.   quest ion
   - ○ c.   que stion
   - ○ d.   question

4. former
   - ○ a.   forme r
   - ○ b.   for mer
   - ○ c.   fo rm er
   - ○ d.   form er

5. perceive
   - ○ a.   perc eive
   - ○ b.   pe rc eive
   - ○ c.   per ceive
   - ○ d.   pe rceive

6. number
   - ○ a.   numb er
   - ○ b.   nu mb er
   - ○ c.   num ber
   - ○ d.   numbe r

7. sector
   - ○ a.   se ct or
   - ○ b.   sec tor
   - ○ c.   se ctor
   - ○ d.   sect or

8. single
   - ○ a.   sin gle
   - ○ b.   sing le
   - ○ c.   si ng le
   - ○ d.   singl e

9. follow
   - ○ a.   fo ll ow
   - ○ b.   foll ow
   - ○ c.   fol low
   - ○ d.   fo llow

10. princess
   - ○ a.   pr in cess
   - ○ b.   pri ncess
   - ○ c.   prin cess
   - ○ d.   princ ess

WORD ATTACK   C. Syllabication   1. *Knows rules for syllables*
g. If a vowel in a syllable is followed by only one consonant, the syllable ends with the vowel

DIRECTIONS: Circle the correct syllabication for each word.

	A	*B*
1. awake	a wake	aw ake
2. radio	ra di o	rad i o
3. even	ev en	e ven
4. water	wa ter	wat er
5. human	hu man	hum an
6. begin	beg in	be gin
7. baby	bab y	ba by
8. beneath	ben eath	be neath
9. open	op en	o pen
10. remove	rem ove	re move

WORD ATTACK   C. Syllabication   **1. *Knows rules for syllables***
g. If a vowel in a syllable is followed by only one consonant, the syllable ends with the vowel

DIRECTIONS: Circle the correct syllabication for each word.

		A	*B*
1.	vapor	va por	vap or
2.	emerge	e merge	em erge
3.	local	loc al	lo cal
4.	mosaic	mos a ic	mo sa ic
5.	amaze	a maze	am aze
6.	about	ab out	a bout
7.	major	ma jor	maj or
8.	detail	det ail	de tail
9.	chosen	cho sen	chos en
10.	moment	mo ment	mom ent

WORD ATTACK   C. Syllabication   1. *Knows rules for syllables*
                                           g. If a vowel in a syllable is followed by only one consonant, the syllable ends with the vowel

DIRECTIONS: Say each of the following words to yourself. Then, write the word, dividing it into syllables.

1. soda   _____

2. stadium   _____

3. delay   _____

4. season   _____

5. defy   _____

6. notice   _____

7. forum   _____

8. private   _____

9. rival   _____

10. before   _____

Name: _____ Date: _____

WORD ATTACK   C. Syllabication   1. *Knows rules for syllables*
g. If a vowel in a syllable is followed by only one consonant, the syllable ends with the vowel

---

DIRECTIONS: Say each of the following words to yourself. Then, write the word, dividing it into syllables.

1. vital   _____

2. fever   _____

3. mural   _____

4. music   _____

5. holy   _____

6. toga   _____

7. tomato   _____

8. meter   _____

9. hotel   _____

10. naval   _____

WORD ATTACK   C. Syllabication   **1. *Knows rules for syllables***
         h. If a word ends in *le*, the consonant just
         before the *l* begins the last syllable

DIRECTIONS: Say the words below to yourself. Then, select and circle the correct syllabication for each.

		A	*B*
1.	gable	ga ble	gab le
2.	idle	id le	i dle
3.	stifle	stif le	sti fle
4.	wiggle	wig gle	wigg le
5.	wrinkle	wrin kle	wrink le
6.	dimple	dim ple	dimp le
7.	hustle	hust le	hus tle
8.	gentle	gent le	gen tle
9.	stumble	stum ble	stumb le
10.	fizzle	fiz zle	fizz le

WORD ATTACK   C. Syllabication   1. *Knows rules for syllables*
                                   h. If a word ends in *le*, the consonant just
                                   before the *l* begins the last syllable

DIRECTIONS: Say the words below to yourself. Then, write each one on the line provided, dividing it into syllables.

1. fumble   _____

2. circle   _____

3. ladle   _____

4. jungle   _____

5. twinkle   _____

6. steeple   _____

7. cradle   _____

8. bottle   _____

9. middle   _____

10. muzzle   _____

WORD ATTACK   **C. Syllabication**   **1. *Knows rules for syllables***
         h. If a word ends in *le*, the consonant just
            before the *l* begins the last syllable

DIRECTIONS: Say the words below to yourself. Then, write each one on the line provided, dividing it into syllables.

1. cobble   _____

2. dawdle   _____

3. needle   _____

4. waffle   _____

5. gargle   _____

6. angle   _____

7. crinkle   _____

8. rumple   _____

9. puzzle   _____

10. cattle   _____

WORD ATTACK   C. Syllabication   1. *Knows rules for syllables*
>   **h.** If a word ends in *le*, the consonant just
>   before the *l* begins the last syllable

DIRECTIONS: Say each word to yourself. Then, fill in the circle in front of the correct syllabication.

1. trouble
   - ○ a.   tr oub le
   - ○ b.   troub le
   - ○ c.   trou ble
   - ○ d.   troubl e

2. particle
   - ○ a.   par tic le
   - ○ b.   par ti cle
   - ○ c.   part i cle
   - ○ d.   par tic le

3. candle
   - ○ a.   can dle
   - ○ b.   cand le
   - ○ c.   c and le
   - ○ d.   candl e

4. gurgle
   - ○ a.   gurg le
   - ○ b.   g urg le
   - ○ c.   gur gle
   - ○ d.   gurgl e

5. sparkle
   - ○ a.   spar kle
   - ○ b.   sp ark le
   - ○ c.   spark le
   - ○ d.   sp arkl e

6. miracle
   - ○ a.   mi ra cle
   - ○ b.   m irac le
   - ○ c.   mir a cle
   - ○ d.   mi rac le

7. people
   - ○ a.   pe op le
   - ○ b.   peo ple
   - ○ c.   peop le
   - ○ d.   people

8. epistle
   - ○ a.   e pis tle
   - ○ b.   ep ist le
   - ○ c.   epi stle
   - ○ d.   epis tle

9. bundle
   - ○ a.   bund le
   - ○ b.   b und le
   - ○ c.   bun dle
   - ○ d.   b undl e

10. whistle
    - ○ a.   wh ist le
    - ○ b.   whist le
    - ○ c.   whis tle
    - ○ d.   whi stle

WORD ATTACK   C. Syllabication   1. *Knows rules for syllables*
         i. When there is an *r* after a vowel, the *r*
         goes with the vowel

DIRECTIONS: Read each word carefully to yourself. Underline the vowel and the *r* affected by the rule stated above. Then, select the correct syllabication for the word and write the letter in the space provided.

		a.	b.	c.
_____	1. corral	corr al	cor ral	co rral
_____	2. barbecue	bar be cue	barb e cue	barb ec ue
_____	3. hurricane	hurri cane	hur ri cane	hur ric ane
_____	4. orator	ora tor	o rat or	or a tor
_____	5. morbid	morb id	mo rb id	mor bid
_____	6. marrow	mar row	marr ow	m ar row
_____	7. transparent	trans pa rent	trans par ent	tran spar ent
_____	8. arrogant	arr o gant	ar ro gant	ar rog ant
_____	9. heroine	he ro ine	hero ine	her o ine
_____	10. humorous	hu mor ous	hum or ous	humor ous

WORD ATTACK   C. Syllabication   1. *Knows rules for syllables*
                                   i. When there is an *r* after a vowel, the *r* goes with the vowel

DIRECTIONS: Rewrite the underlined words in the sentences below, dividing them into syllables on the line provided.

1. Yellow checkered <u>curtains</u> were chosen for the kitchen.   _____

2. "Hark the <u>herald</u> angels sing!" are words from a popular Christmas carol.   _____

3. One man stayed in <u>orbit</u> while the others explored the surface of the planet.   _____

4. What is the sense in having a <u>burglar</u> alarm if you don't turn it on?   _____

5. The walls of the empty warehouse <u>reverberate</u> the voices of the viewers.   _____

6. Time erases the memories of even the most <u>horrible</u> experiences.   _____

7. You will succeed in <u>proportion</u> to your efforts.   _____

8. Marinated <u>herring</u> and sardines are often served in fish restaurants.   _____

9. A colorful sunset, an angry sea, and trees bowing in the wind are all <u>marvels</u> to see.   _____

WORD ATTACK   **C. Syllabication**   **1. *Knows rules for syllables***

       i. When there is an *r* after a vowel, the *r* goes with the vowel

DIRECTIONS: Read each word listed below carefully to yourself. Underline the vowel and the *r* affected by the rule stated above. Then, select the correct syllabication for the word and write the letter in the space provided.

		a.	b.	c.
_____	1. derby	derb y	der by	d er by
_____	2. garden	g ard en	gard en	gar den
_____	3. market	mar ket	mark et	m ark et
_____	4. cursive	curs ive	c urs ive	cur sive
_____	5. corridor	cor ri dor	corr i dor	corrid or
_____	6. burden	burd en	bur den	b ur den
_____	7. gallery	gal ler y	ga ller y	gall er y
_____	8. corsage	cors age	cor sage	c or sage
_____	9. moderate	mo der ate	mod er ate	mode rate
_____	10. tolerate	to ler ate	tol er ate	tole rate

WORD ATTACK   C. Syllabication   1. *Knows rules for syllables*
                                   i. When there is an *r* after a vowel, the *r*
                                      goes with the vowel

DIRECTIONS: In each of the words listed below, underline the vowel and the *r* affected by the rule stated above. Read the word carefully to yourself. Then, write the word divided into syllables on the line provided.

1. barber   _____

2. error   _____

3. hurtle   _____

4. literary   _____

5. hurry   _____

6. curdle   _____

7. merit   _____

8. terrace   _____

9. orphan   _____

10. numerous   _____

WORD ATTACK   **D. Knows Accent Rules**
        1. *In a word of two or more syllables, the first syllable is usually accented unless it is a prefix*

DIRECTIONS: In each row, draw a circle around the word in which the beginning syllable is not accented.

	A	B	C
1.	about	terror	process
2.	method	appear	cargo
3.	visitor	living	requirement
4.	image	sublime	chemical
5.	tidy	review	satisfy
6.	incorrect	wetness	peasant
7.	lawyer	sculpture	diplomat
8.	picture	guidance	again
9.	remove	continent	guidance
10.	battle	invert	pattern

WORD ATTACK   **D. Knows Accent Rules**
           1. *In a word of two or more syllables, the first syllable*
              is usually accented unless it is a prefix

DIRECTIONS: Read the word at the beginning of each line. Then, circle the word that is correctly accented.

	A	*B*
1. during	dur ing′	dur′ ing
2. inept	in′ ept	in ept′
3. civil	civ il′	civ′ il
4. behold	be′ hold	be hold′
5. punish	pun ish′	pun′ ish
6. trailer	trail′ er	trail er′
7. mystery	mys′ ter y	mys ter′ y
8. reopen	re′ o pen	re o′ pen
9. pennant	pen′ nant	pen nant′
10. enter	en ter′	en′ ter

WORD ATTACK   **D. Knows Accent Rules**
1. *In a word of two or more syllables, the first syllable is usually accented unless it is a prefix*

DIRECTIONS: Place an accent mark on the proper syllable for each of the words below.

1. gallery   gal ler y

2. event   e vent

3. surface   sur face

4. peasant   peas ant

5. beware   be ware

6. report   re port

7. positive   pos i tive

8. method   meth od

9. resistance   re sist ance

10. prefer   pre fer

WORD ATTACK   **D. Knows Accent Rules**

   1. *In a word of two or more syllables, the first syllable is usually accented unless it is a prefix*

DIRECTIONS: Rewrite each word below, breaking it into syllables and placing an accent mark on the correct syllable.

1. living   _____

2. enter   _____

3. vanish   _____

4. portrait   _____

5. tatter   _____

6. rivet   _____

7. lion   _____

8. dinner   _____

9. universe   _____

10. flatter   _____

WORD ATTACK   D. Knows Accent Rules
2. *In most two-syllable words that end in a consonant followed by y, the first syllable is accented and the last is unaccented*

DIRECTIONS: There are two words in each row. On the line provided for each word, write *C* if the word is correctly accented and *X* if the word is not correctly accented.

1. ti′ dy   _____   mal′ a dy   _____

2. mag ni fy′   _____   air′ y   _____

3. mar′ ry   _____   man′ gy   _____

4. pal try′   _____   pi ra′ cy   _____

5. saint′ ly   _____   late′ ly   _____

6. ti ny′   _____   cen′ tu ry   _____

7. am′ nes ty   _____   bag gy′   _____

8. sil′ ly   _____   brin′ y   _____

9. bush′ y   _____   can ny′   _____

10. i′ cy   _____   live′ ly   _____

Name: _____ Date: _____

WORD ATTACK   D. Knows Accent Rules
      2. *In most two-syllable words that end in a consonant followed by y, the first syllable is accented and the last is unaccented*

DIRECTIONS: Read the word at the beginning of each line. Then, circle the word that is correctly accented.

	A	B
1. buggy	bug gy′	bug′ gy
2. mystery	mys′ ter y	mys ter′ y
3. musky	musk′ y	musk y′
4. holly	hol ly′	hol′ ly
5. daddy	dad′ dy	dad dy′
6. early	ear′ ly	ear ly′
7. baby	ba by′	ba′ by
8. brainy	brain′ y	brain y′
9. army	ar my′	ar′ my
10. allergy	al′ ler gy	al ler gy′

WORD ATTACK   **D. Knows Accent Rules**

2. *In most two-syllable words that end in a consonant*
followed by y, the first syllable is accented and the
last is unaccented

DIRECTIONS: Put the accent on the proper syllable in each of the words below.

1. baggy   bag gy

2. burglary   bur glar y

3. candy   can dy

4. century   cen tu ry

5. fish   fish y

6. clumsy   clum sy

7. likely   like ly

8. tally   tal ly

9. bounty   boun ty

10. dimity   dim i ty

WORD ATTACK   **D. Knows Accent Rules**
                   2. *In most two-syllable words that end in a consonant*
                   followed by y, the first syllable is accented and the
                   last is unaccented

DIRECTIONS: In the sentences below, divide each word of two or more syllables into syllables and put the accent mark on the correct syllable.

1. The brainy lawyer will certify the equipment.

2. Picture an army, intent and busy.

3. The battle was about civil guidance.

4. The bully was lofty, lonely, and cranky.

5. A flashy lady rode on a bushy pony.

6. The cabby was in a fury when the furry thing caused him to brake.

7. Winter: holly berries? Yes. Balmy and breezy? No.

8. Sticky candy left on the sidewalk made my brawny buddy angry.

9. A bulky and canny gypsy deals in mystery.

10. The fog that hides the holy belfry is cloudy and chilly.

WORD ATTACK   **D. Knows Accent Rules**
     3. *Beginning syllables* de, re, be, er, in, *and* a *are usually not accented*

DIRECTIONS: In each row, circle the word in which the beginning syllable is not accented.

	A	*B*	*C*
1.	ajar	tender	travel
2.	ability	senile	render
3.	label	erupt	hilly
4.	petty	deceit	pewter
5.	pebble	relic	reveal
6.	indecent	hocus	hiccup
7.	error	begonia	hindrance
8.	bewitch	satisfy	simple
9.	silver	pedal	abominate
10.	revival	liar	basket

WORD ATTACK   D. Knows Accent Rules
   3. Beginning syllables de, re, be, er, in, *and* a *are usually not accented*

DIRECTIONS: There are two words in each row. On the line provided for each word, write *C* if the word is correctly accented and *X* if the word is not correctly accented.

1. a loud′	_____	de duct′	_____
2. er rand′	_____	e rase′	_____
3. de ci′ sion	_____	des′ ti ny	_____
4. re′ sent	_____	res′ i dence	_____
5. in sane′	_____	in′ va sion	_____
6. a′ board	_____	de cap′ i tate	_____
7. in′ deed	_____	be hind′	_____
8. re mark′	_____	re mem′ ber	_____
9. in flate′	_____	in fu′ ri ate	_____
10. re′ pose	_____	in′ struc tion	_____

WORD ATTACK   **D. Knows Accent Rules**

           3. *Beginning syllables* **de, re, be, er, in,** *and* **a** *are usually not accented*

DIRECTIONS: Put the accent on the correct syllable for the words below.

1. agreeable	a gree a ble
2. December	De cem ber
3. arrogant	ar ro gant
4. defeat	de feat
5. retirement	re tire ment
6. indifferent	in dif fer ent
7. different	dif fer ent
8. beside	be side
9. resort	re sort
10. abolish	a bol ish

Name: _____ Date: _____

D. Knows Accent Rules
     3. *Beginning syllables* de, re, be, er, in, *and* a *are usually not accented*

DIRECTIONS: Rewrite the words below, dividing them into syllables and placing an accent mark on the correct syllable.

1. ablaze   _____

2. absence   _____

3. erode   _____

4. degree   _____

5. resume   _____

6. include   _____

7. believe   _____

8. belfry   _____

9. benign   _____

10. delicious   _____

WORD ATTACK   **D. Knows Accent Rules**
      3. Beginning syllables de, re, be, er, in, *and* a *are usually not accented*

DIRECTIONS: In the sentences below, divide each word of two or more syllables into syllables and put the accent mark on the correct syllable.

1. The defect in the alarm informed the cabby.

2. When against a defiant rebel, try retreat.

3. Along with decay, erosion arouses caring persons.

4. The door of the abode was left ajar and declared it empty.

5. Reside inside beside agreeable me.

6. Hilly land abloom invites a weary lady to repose.

7. A report of decrease in instruction again awakens fury of bemoaning parents.

8. Alerts to deceitful revolver-hiding burglars decrease crime.

9. Alike and unafraid, the twins decide on deception to bewilder and infuriate.

10. Remember: betray not; invade not; defame not.

WORD ATTACK   **D. Knows Accent Rules**
               4. *When a suffix is added, the accent falls on or within the root word*

DIRECTIONS: For each word below, draw a line through the incorrectly accented example.

	A	B
1. weakly	weak ly′	weak′ ly
2. beautiful	beau′ ti ful	beau ti ful′
3. repairable	re′ pair a ble	re pair′ a ble
4. glorious	glo′ ri ous	glo ri′ ous
5. metallic	me tal lic′	me tal′ lic
6. abundance	a bun dance′	a bun′ dance
7. voltage	volt′ age	volt age′
8. itemize	i′ tem ize	i tem′ ize
9. regardless	re′ gard less	re gard′ less
10. friendship	friend′ ship	friend ship′

WORD ATTACK   **D. Knows Accent Rules**
     **4. *When a suffix is added, the accent falls on or within
          the root word***

DIRECTIONS: For each word below, circle the example that is correctly accented.

		A	*B*
1.	injustice	in jus' tice	in' jus tice
2.	veteran	vet er' an	vet' er an
3.	insular	in sul' ar	in' sul ar
4.	fatherhood	fa' ther hood	fa ther' hood
5.	vocally	vo cal' ly	vo' cal ly
6.	meddlesome	med' dle some	med dle' some
7.	acreage	a cre' age	a' cre age
8.	scrimmage	scrim' mage	scrim mage'
9.	statesmanship	states man' ship	states' man ship
10.	elector	e lec' tor	e' lec tor

WORD ATTACK   **D. Knows Accent Rules**
                  4. When a suffix is added, the accent falls on or within
                     the root word

DIRECTIONS: For each word below, place an accent mark on the correct syllable.

1. glamorous   glam or ous

2. Arabic   Ar a bic

3. itemize   i tem ize

4. completely   com plete ly

5. conspirator   con spir a tor

6. portable   port a ble

7. contentment   con tent ment

8. seaward   sea ward

9. delightful   de light ful

10. adjuster   ad just er

WORD ATTACK   D. Knows Accent Rules
                    4. When a suffix is added, the accent falls on or within
                       the root word

DIRECTIONS: In the sentences below, divide each word of two or more syllables into syllables and put the accent mark on the correct syllable.

1. History will report perilous heroics.

2. Purity of speech reveals effort.

3. The bony jumper will decide the race.

4. Foggy days retard departing planes.

5. Snow removal lengthens the custodian's day.

6. The head runner kept a respectful lead.

7. Insect repellent was not effective.

8. His sculpture was a handsome, lifelike likeness.

9. It will abolish coverage of falsehoods.

10. Friendship finds incredible bounty effortless.

WORD ATTACK   D. Knows Accent Rules
        4. *When a suffix is added, the accent falls on or within*
            the root word

DIRECTIONS: Read the following words to yourself. Then, rewrite each word, breaking it into syllables and placing an accent mark on the correct syllable.

1. placement   _____

2. suggestion   _____

3. shapeless   _____

4. endurance   _____

5. unforgettable _____

6. forward   _____

7. progressive   _____

8. dangerous   _____

9. nervousness   _____

10. purity   _____

WORD ATTACK   **D. Knows Accent Rules**
                    5. Endings that form syllables are usually unaccented

DIRECTIONS: For each word below, circle the example that is correctly accented.

		A	*B*
1.	downward	down ward′	down′ ward
2.	manhole	man hole′	man′ hole
3.	nylon	ny′ lon	ny lon′
4.	pickup	pick′ up	pick up′
5.	backbone	back bone′	back′ bone
6.	pickaback	pick′ a back	pick a′ back
7.	axiom	ax′ i om	ax i om′
8.	letterhead	let ter′ head	let′ ter head
9.	acetate	ac e tate′	ac′ e tate
10.	songster	song′ ster	song ster′

Name: _____ Date: _____

DIRECTIONS: In each row, draw a line through the word that is incorrectly accented.

	A	*B*	*C*
1.	girl′ hood	up′ ward	eye wash′
2.	line man′	old′ ster	fish′ tail
3.	self ish′	some′ where	lone′ some
4.	king′ dom	non′ sense	kid nap′
5.	un′ der brush	cap size′	hand′ i cap
6.	out′ side	head line′	walk′ out
7.	way side′	tat too′	ver′ dict
8.	les′ son	ice man′	car′ ton
9.	cap′ tain	head long′	fol′ de rol
10.	side′ track	hold up′	tooth′ ache

WORD ATTACK   **D. Knows Accent Rules**
                  5. *Endings that form syllables are usually unaccented*

DIRECTIONS: If the word is accented correctly, write *C* in the space provided. If it is incorrect, write *X*.

1. snowfall   ——————   snow fall′

2. thereabouts   ——————   there′ a bouts

3. hopelessness   ——————   hope′ less ness

4. someone   ——————   some′ one

5. adjust   ——————   ad′ just

6. armpit   ——————   arm pit′

7. thunderstruck   ——————   thun′ der struck

8. lettuce   ——————   let tuce′

9. omen   ——————   o′ men

10. uppermost   ——————   up′ per most

WORD ATTACK   D. Knows Accent Rules
                5. *Endings that form syllables are usually unaccented*

DIRECTIONS: For each word below, place an accent mark on the correct syllable.

1. boardwalk   board walk

2. brotherhood   bro ther hood

3. sonny   son ny

4. domino   dom i no

5. senselessness   sense less ness

6. folklore   folk lore

7. illegal   il le gal

8. bonehead   bone head

9. heavenward   heav en ward

10. manifold   man i fold

WORD ATTACK   **D. Knows Accent Rules**
                 5. *Endings that form syllables are usually unaccented*

DIRECTIONS: Read each of the following words to yourself. Then, on the line provided, divide the word into syllables and place an accent mark on the correct syllable.

1. folderol   _____

2. whereabouts   _____

3. kinsfolk   _____

4. tailback   _____

5. womanhood   _____

6. tonsil   _____

7. toothless   _____

8. menace   _____

9. sideline   _____

10. corkscrew   _____

Name: _____ Date: _____

                        6. *When a final syllable ends in* le, *that syllable is usually not accented*

DIRECTIONS: For each word below, circle the example that is correctly accented.

		A	B
1.	possible	pos' si ble	pos si' ble
2.	available	a vail a' ble	a vail' a ble
3.	supple	sup' ple	sup ple'
4.	recycle	re' cy cle	re cy' cle
5.	rifle	ri' fle	ri fle'
6.	incredible	in cred i' ble	in cred' i ble
7.	title	ti tle'	ti' tle
8.	scramble	scram' ble	scram ble'
9.	enkindle	en' kin dle	en kin' dle
10.	bugle	bu' gle	bu gle'

WORD ATTACK   **D. Knows Accent Rules**
                   ***6. When a final syllable ends in** le, **that syllable is
                       usually not accented***

DIRECTIONS: Say each word to yourself. Then, fill in the circle in front of the example that is correctly accented.

1. feeble

   ○ a. fee' ble
   ○ b. fee ble'
   ○ c. fee' ble'

2. guzzle

   ○ a. guz zle'
   ○ b. guz' zle'
   ○ c. guz' zle

3. table

   ○ a. ta ble'
   ○ b. ta' ble
   ○ c. ta' ble'

4. projectile

   ○ a. pro jec' tile
   ○ b. pro' jec tile
   ○ c. pro jec tile'

5. gamble

   ○ a. gam ble'
   ○ b. gam' ble
   ○ c. gam' ble'

6. example

   ○ a. ex' am ple
   ○ b. ex am' ple
   ○ c. ex am ple'

7. comfortable

   ○ a. com for' ta ble
   ○ b. com' for ta ble
   ○ c. com for ta ble'

8. wrestle

   ○ a. wres' tle
   ○ b. wres tle'
   ○ c. wres' tle'

9. eligible

   ○ a. el i gi' ble
   ○ b. el' i gi ble
   ○ c. el i' gi ble

10. double

   ○ a. dou' ble
   ○ b. dou ble'
   ○ c. dou' ble'

WORD ATTACK   D. Knows Accent Rules
      6. *When a final syllable ends in* le, *that syllable is usually not accented*

DIRECTIONS: For each word below, place an accent mark on the correct syllable.

1. flexible   flex i ble

2. humble   hum ble

3. finagle   fi na gle

4. giggle   gig gle

5. automobile   au to mo bile

6. infantile   in fan tile

7. passable   pass a ble

8. triple   tri ple

9. assemble   as sem ble

10. bicycle   bi cy cle

WORD ATTACK   **D. Knows Accent Rules**
                    6. *When a final syllable ends in* le, *that syllable is usually not accented*

DIRECTIONS: Read each of the following words to yourself. Then, on the line provided, write the word divided into syllables with the correct accent mark.

1. idle   _____

2. huddle   _____

3. divisible   _____

4. particle   _____

5. gentle   _____

6. entangle   _____

7. waggle   _____

8. operable   _____

9. globule   _____

10. axle   _____

WORD ATTACK   D. Knows Accent Rules
                6. *When a final syllable ends in* le, *that syllable is usually not accented*

DIRECTIONS: In the sentences below, divide each word of two or more syllables into syllables and put the accent mark on the correct syllable for each.

1. The people guzzle and whistle.

2. To ride a bicycle is simple.

3. Handle wattles with care.

4. Single or double chords are hard to play on a fiddle.

5. The ensemble fizzled.

6. The bridle path will encircle the seaward road.

7. The gentle maiden dreams of a fanciful caper.

8. Struggle and trouble are part of the scramble to live.

9. The stagestruck player was in a flashy role.

10. Multiple shuttle vans will carry plucky kids up the hilly road.

WORD ATTACK   E. Knows Possessives

DIRECTIONS: Write the possessive form for each of the following phrases.

1. The followers of the president

   _____

2. The clowning of the football player

   _____

3. The decision of the umpire

   _____

4. The wings of the bats

   _____

5. The brother of Phyllis and the son of James

   _____

6. The patience of the teacher

   _____

7. The wisdom of the aged leader

   _____

8. The champions of democracy

   _____

9. The misfortunes of Charlie

   _____

10. The strike of the actors

   _____

WORD ATTACK   E. Knows Possessives

DIRECTIONS: Rewrite the following sentences using possessives. Each answer should be one sentence.

1. The fruit basket had contents. The contents were ripe and sweet.

   _____

2. The signal of the searchers was awaited with anxiety.

   _____

3. The new suit my mother has is a popular color this season.

   _____

4. The thermometer has mercury. The mercury is down to zero.

   _____

5. Amy has a book bag. The bag has the face of a clown on it.

   _____

6. Nathan has ice skates. They are dull and need sharpening.

   _____

7. Mabel had a story. It was fantastic and very funny.

   _____

8. Gus had his homework. It disappeared from his desk.

   _____

9. Andrew has a red sports car. It gets twenty-five miles per gallon.

   _____

10. The interstate highway has a good safety record. The record improved with the lower speed limit.

   _____

WORD ATTACK   E. Knows Possessives

DIRECTIONS: Rewrite the following sentences using possessives. Each answer should be one sentence.

1. The book has a title. The title is *Stories of Faith*.

_____

2. Burn victims have scars. These fade with time.

_____

3. San Francisco has cable cars. These are both a tourist attraction and a means of transportation.

_____

4. The carpet cleaner has a powerful machine. It cleans quickly and well.

_____

5. The car had a faulty generator. It caused a breakdown.

_____

6. The balance of the checkbook did not coincide with the bank statements.

_____

7. The ending of the film brought loud applause.

_____

8. The mailman had trousers. The Smiths had a dog who tore them.

_____

9. The marathon racer was exhausted. The exhaustion slowed his pace.

_____

10. The crowd yelled. The yells upset the batter.

_____

WORD ATTACK   E. Knows Possessives   175

DIRECTIONS: Rewrite the following sentences using possessives. Each answer should be one sentence.

1. The candidates made speeches. They were rip-roaring.

    _____

2. The artist had a palette. It was a blurb of colors.

    _____

3. The ruler had a ragged edge. It cut my thumb.

    _____

4. The village has many antique shops. The shops are filled with quaint and curious things.

    _____

5. The tour guide made comments. The comments were interesting.

    _____

6. Motorcycle riders have helmets. The helmets are for safety.

    _____

7. The city library has a record collection. The collection includes popular and classical music.

    _____

8. Police cars have flashing lights. The lights demand the right of way.

    _____

9. St. Louis has a gateway arch. This arch recalls the history of the city as the gateway to the West.

    _____

10. School athletes receive letters. The letters indicate the sport in which they participated.

    _____

WORD ATTACK   E. Knows Possessives

DIRECTIONS: Rewrite the following sentences using the possessive form for the underlined words.

1. <u>The father of the seven sisters</u> was ninety years old.

   _____

2. Geologists flew over <u>the crater of the volcano</u>.

   _____

3. Mr. Short painted <u>the desk of his child</u>.

   _____

4. Everyone went swimming in <u>the pool of the boss</u>.

   _____

5. You cannot tell <u>the contents of a book</u> by <u>the cover of the book</u>.

   _____

6. <u>The tails of the three dogs</u> kept wagging.

   _____

7. Kevin insisted he had not heard <u>the request of his mother</u>.

   _____

8. Jane denied seeing <u>the cat of her sister</u>.

   _____

9. <u>The forecast of the weatherman</u> was accurate.

   _____

10. Thrown rocks cracked <u>the windshield of the car</u>.

    _____

WORD ATTACK   **F. Knows Contractions**   177

DIRECTIONS: Write out the full words for each of the following contractions.

     1. It's great!   _____

     2. I'd like to.   _____

     3. That can't be!   _____

     4. I'd forgotten.   _____

     5. She hasn't come.   _____

     6. He didn't know.   _____

     7. They're all wet.   _____

     8. They'll be late again.   _____

     9. We've remembered.   _____

    10. The dog wouldn't bark.   _____

WORD ATTACK   F. Knows Contractions

DIRECTIONS: Write the contraction for each pair of words underlined.

1. He <u>will not</u> be a candidate.   _____

2. She <u>is not</u> tired.   _____

3. We <u>do not</u> have the time.   _____

4. Mother <u>has not</u> lost hope.   _____

5. That <u>had not</u> occurred to me.   _____

6. They <u>have not</u> eaten the candy.   _____

7. <u>We will</u> be ready.   _____

8. <u>It will</u> be all right.   _____

9. You <u>could not</u> come then.   _____

10. <u>She is</u> absent again.   _____

WORD ATTACK   F. Knows Contractions

DIRECTIONS: Write the contraction for each pair of words underlined.

1. He had better study!   _____

2. She will leave Friday.   _____

3. I will cry tomorrow.   _____

4. They have just arrived.   _____

5. It is a pity!   _____

6. We would like to go.   _____

7. We had just left.   _____

8. I have a better idea.   _____

9. You will regret not studying.   _____

10. You have won!   _____

WORD ATTACK   F. Knows Contractions

DIRECTIONS: Write out the full words for each of the following contractions.

1. I'm so happy!   _____

2. He shouldn't worry.   _____

3. That wasn't funny.   _____

4. We're in the money.   _____

5. He's an old stick-in-the-mud.   _____

6. I shan't fail.   _____

7. It really doesn't matter.   _____

8. You'd better hurry.   _____

9. They'd better think twice.   _____

10. You've no time to lose.   _____

WORD ATTACK   F. Knows Contractions   181

DIRECTIONS: A. Write out the full word for each of the contractions.

1. That's an experience we're not likely to
   forget.   _____

2. They hadn't gone a mile when the tire went
   flat.   _____

3. Bob's parents weren't about to buy him a
   gun.   _____

4. You'd be happier if you worked harder.   _____

5. You've forgotten your promise.   _____

DIRECTIONS: B. Form contractions for the underlined words.

6. It will rain tomorrow.   _____

7. She would stay if she could.   _____

8. Do not touch.   _____

9. Money does not buy happiness.   _____

10. We will win!   _____

WORD ATTACK   G. Knows Silent Letters

DIRECTIONS: Say each of the following words to yourself. If there are any silent letters in the word, cross them out. If no letter is silent, leave the word as it is.

1. sight

2. wring

3. knot

4. thumb

5. gush

6. gherkin

7. knee

8. gnarl

9. bomb

10. thought

11. know

12. wreck

WORD ATTACK   G. Knows Silent Letters

DIRECTIONS: Some letters have been crossed out in the following words. If the letter crossed out is the one that is not pronounced in the word, put a *C* for *correct* on the line next to the word. If the letter crossed out should be pronounced, rewrite the word with the proper letter crossed out.

1. leøpard   _____

2. kn̸ew   _____

3. ẃriter   _____

4. ẃrangler   _____

5. g̸nash   _____

6. K̸navé   _____

7. comb̸   _____

8. gh̸ost   _____

9. damn̸ed   _____

10. pl̸umbing   _____

11. K̸night   _____

12. ẃeird   _____

WORD ATTACK   G. Knows Silent Letters

DIRECTIONS: Some letters have been crossed out in the following words. If the letter crossed out is the one that is not pronounced in that word, put a *C* for *correct* on the line next to the word. If the letter crossed out should be pronounced, rewrite the word with the proper letter crossed out.

1. lim~~e~~   _____

2. ~~t~~icktock   _____

3. g~~h~~ost   _____

4. bu~~t~~cher   _____

5. w~~r~~eath   _____

6. k~~n~~if~~e~~   _____

7. ~~w~~ren   _____

8. lam~~b~~   _____

9. k~~n~~apsa~~c~~k   _____

10. ri~~g~~ht   _____

11. dou~~gh~~nut   _____

12. thro~~w~~   _____

WORD ATTACK   G. **Knows Silent Letters**   185

DIRECTIONS: Say each of the following words to yourself. If there are any silent letters in the word, cross them out. If no letter is silent, leave the word as it is.

1. ghetto

2. plumb

3. pitcher

4. gnaw

5. knack

6. wrap

7. portray

8. solemn

9. straight

10. toast

11. ruler

12. numb

WORD ATTACK   G. Knows Silent Letters

DIRECTIONS: Say each of the following words to yourself. If there are any silent letters in the word, cross them out. If no letter is silent, leave the word as it is.

1. pitch

2. gnu

3. dumb

4. kneeler

5. column

6. bough

7. lumber

8. conscience

9. plague

10. knickers

11. plumber

12. shoulder

WORD ATTACK   H. Knows Glossary

DIRECTIONS: There are ten sentences below. Use the information you get from the mini glossary here. Then, cross out the word or words that are incorrect in each sentence.

fas ces (făs′ ēz), a bundle of rods with an axe in the center; for the Romans, a symbol of power, 80.

fo rum (fôr′ əm), in Rome, place where stood the government buildings and temples; a market or public place in a city, 6-8.

glad i a tor (glăd′ ē ā tər), in Rome, usually a slave or captive, armed, compelled to fight to the death to entertain the people, 20.

Lat in (lăt′ ′n), the language spoken in ancient Rome, see Latium.

Lat ins (lăt′ ′ns), people who lived in ancient Latium, whom the Romans conquered.

La ti um (lā′ shē əm), plains area southeast of Rome settled by the Latins, 65.

le gion (lē′ jən), 3000 to 6000 foot soldiers who were the backbone of the Roman army, 80.

pa ter (pā′ tər), the father of the Roman family, the male head of the household, who ruled as lord and master, 29.

pa tri cian (pa trish′ ən), a member of the highest ruling class of Rome, 55, see aristocracy.

trib unes (trib′ yōonz), Romans elected to protect the rights and interests of the lowest class, 40, see plebs.

1. A   male/female   head of a Roman household was called *pater*.

2. Tribunes were   elected/appointed   officials.

3. To win wars/To entertain the people   was the task of the gladiators.

4. When a Roman wanted to meet friends or find out the latest news, he went to the tribune/forum.

5. There are   three/four   syllables in the word *patrician*.

6. In ancient Rome, the language spoken was   Roman/Latin.

7. The fasces were   a political party/a symbol of power.

8. Patricians/Slaves   were forced to fight to the death to entertain.

9. Aristocracy/Plebs   should be associated with tribunes.

10. To learn more about patricians, you should refer to the word   *plebs/aristocracy.*

WORD ATTACK   **H. Knows Glossary**

DIRECTIONS: Using the mini glossary provided here, find the information for each of the underlined words and write it on the line provided below.

al tim e ter (ăl tĭm′ ə tər), instrument used on aircraft to show height above the earth's surface, 28.

bi plane (bī′ plān), airplane with two sets of wings, one above the other, 99.

blimp (blimp), small gas-filled airship looking like a balloon which can be guided or steered, 76.

de scent (dĭ sĕnt′), movement down from a higher to a lower level, 64.

fu se lage (fyōō′ sə läzh), body of an airplane containing engine and controls but without wings and other parts attached, 39.

hang ar (hăng′ ər), building for storing aircraft, 43.

pro pel ler (prə pĕl′ ər), device with two or more blades attached to the center of a wheel; its circular motion causes an airplane or ship to move forward, 74.

rud der (rŭd′ ər), flat piece of wood or metal hung up and down by hinges to the sternpost of a ship or plane and used for steering.

vis i bil i ty (vĭz ə bĭl′ ə tē), distance from which one can see or be seen, 16.

1. A glance at the *altimeter* alerted the pilot to trouble. *Meaning:* _____

   _____

2. The Graf Zeppelin was a huge *blimp. On what page?* _____

3. When flying from Atlanta to New York at 30,000 feet, *descent* begins over

   Philadelphia. *Syllabication:* _____ *Page:* _____

4. Stripped of its wings, the *fuselage* looked strange.

   Definition: _____

5. *Hangars* have giant doors that look like walls. *Pronunciation:* _____

   Definition: _____

6. *Propeller*-driven planes have given way to jets. *Number of syllables:* _____

   Syllabication: _____

7. The pilot had difficulty getting the plane to its gate because its *rudder* was damaged.

   Definition: _____

8. Without instruments, when *visibility* is under one mile, planes are forbidden to land or

   take off. *Number of syllables:* _____

   Meaning: _____

9. On early *biplanes,* struts were in plain sight. *Page:* _____

   Definition: _____

WORD ATTACK   H. Knows Glossary

DIRECTIONS: Using information from the mini glossary here, answer the questions that appear below.

am phib i an (ăm fĭb′ ē ən), a cold-blooded animal that can live in water and on land, 80, 101.
a nat o my (ə năt′ ə mē), the science that deals with the structure of the human body and other living things, 30.
av a lanche (ăv′ ə lănch), the sudden sliding of a mass of snow, ice, rocks, earth, etc., down a mountain slope, 63.
bi ol o gist (bī äl′ ə jĭst), a scientist who studies all forms of life, 19, see also biology.
bot a ny (bät′ 'n ē), the science of plants, their forms, structure, classification, etc., 17.
bra chi al (brāk′ ē əl), pertaining to the arm, 88.

1. How many syllables does the word *biologist* have? _____

2. On what page will you find the word *brachial* used? _____

3. Where would you look for more related information on *biologist*?

_____

4. Define *avalanche*: _____

5. What word relates to your arm? _____

6. In what kind of book would you find information about elm trees? _____

7. How many syllables are in the word *anatomy*? _____

8. On what page or pages is *amphibian* used? _____

9. Name an animal that fits the definition of an *amphibian:*

_____

10. If a *biologist* studies biology, what would you call a person who studies *botany*?

_____

WORD ATTACK   H. Knows Glossary

DIRECTIONS: Use the mini glossary here to find the answers to the questions below.

cel lu lar (sĕl' yŏŏ lər), pertaining to or characterized by cells or units of living matter, 50.

com pres sor (kəm prĕs' ər), a pump or machine that makes the volume of air or gases smaller and increases the pressure, 65.

de lir i um (dĭ lĭr' ē əm), a temporary state during which the mental abilities are in disorder, confused, 72.

ge ol o gy (jē äl'ə jē), science that deals with the history of the origin and makeup of the earth, 88.

gla cier (glā' shər), a very slowly moving mass of ice and snow in areas where snow outlasts the usual melting of the summer, 61.

her pe tol o gist (hûr pə täl' ə jĭst), a scientist who studies amphibians and reptiles, 68.

1. On what page is the word *delirium* to be found? _____

2. How many syllables does *herpetologist* have? _____

3. Which definition relates to volume and pressure? _____

4. When a person is ill with a very high fever and speaks strangely or attempts to do odd things, what state is that person in? _____

5. What scientist would be likely to know about volcanoes? _____

6. What kind of temperature would you find near a *glacier*? _____

7. Which definition deals with information about the earth? _____

8. What does the *herpetologist* study? _____

9. What word should you use to describe something that looks like cells?

_____

WORD ATTACK   H. Knows Glossary

DIRECTIONS: Using the mini glossary below, briefly give the information requested.

aurora borealis (ô rôr' ə bôr ē ăl' is), a phenomenon of bands and streams of light which appears at night in the Northern Hemisphere, 126, see also northern lights.
heritage (hĕr' ə tij), that which one receives by reason of birth, 99.
hydroelectric (hī drə i lĕk' trik), electric energy generated by water power, 120.
igloo (ig' loo), dome-shaped hut built of blocks of hard snow used as house by Eskimos, 112.
lichen (lī' kən), plant composed of fungus and alga which forms on rocks and trees, 98.
lock (läk), an enclosed chamber in a canal with gates at each end for raising or lowering vessels from one level to another by letting water in or out, 90.
maritime (măr' ə tīm), on, near, or living on the sea, 88.
prairie (prĕr' ē), an extensive, level, mostly treeless land, usually with fertile soil, 110.
topography (tə päg' rə fē), the surface features of the earth or of a particular region, including mountains, rivers, valleys, etc., 116.
tun dra (tŭn' drə), vast, almost level, treeless plain of the arctic regions, 118.

1. What kind of energy is generated by falling water? _____

2. Give another name for *aurora borealis*: _____

3. A *prairie* is _____ and a *tundra* is not.

4. Define *lock* from this glossary: _____

5. Something that is received by reason of birth is found on page _____.

6. A description of the hills, valleys, mountains, rivers, brooks, and plains of any area is

   its _____.

7. The Canadian provinces bordering on the Atlantic are _____.

8. Eskimos use _____ to build their _____.

9. What plant forms and grows on rocks and trees? _____

COMPREHENSION   A. Outlining   1. *Takes notes effectively*

DIRECTIONS: Read the following selection and complete the outline form.

Fairies

Many books tell tales about fairies. The stories fascinate and entertain us because a fairy is not a human being. Fairies are supernatural, beyond human beings. They have special powers of magic and enchantment.

From very early times, belief in fairies has existed. Stories of fairies and their experiences with humans are found in the literatures of all nations.

All fairies do not appear the same to all men. Some fit the description of tiny, wizened-faced old men like the Irish leprechaun; some are beautiful enchantresses who lure men to their deaths, like Morgan le Fay and the Lorelei; some, like the giant in "Jack and the Beanstalk," are hideous, man-eating giants or ogres.

Frequently, it was felt that fairies resided in a kingdom of their own. Gnomes, for instance, were thought to reside underground; mermaids lived in the sea; others stayed in an enchanted part of the forest or in some faraway land.

Almost all peoples have fairies in their folklore. The Arabs have jinns, the Scandinavians have trolls, the Germans have elves, and the English have pixies.

I.   Fairies

    A. Definition   D. Residences

        1.   1.

        2.   2.

                              3.

    B. Existence   E. Kinds

        1.   1.

        2.   2.

                              3.

    C. Descriptions   4.

        1.

        2.

        3.

COMPREHENSION   A. Outlining   1. *Takes notes effectively*

DIRECTIONS: Read the following selection and complete the outline form.

Prairies

When the word "prairie" is mentioned, the picture that comes to mind is that of flat and treeless land for miles and miles, far beyond what the eye can see. Prairies are the plains of North America.

To easterners, far westerners, and southerners, "prairie" is a word in a book. Prairies are, however, a familiar sight to the people who inhabit the middle section of the United States. The prairies stretch from western Ohio, through Indiana, Illinois, and Iowa, to the Great Plains region which begins on the western shore of the Mississippi River and rises very gradually to the foothills of the Rocky Mountains. The prairie belt also extends into northern Missouri, southern Michigan, Wisconsin, Minnesota, the eastern part of North and South Dakota, and southern Canada.

Formerly, the prairies were used for grazing. They are gradually coming under cultivation, and no wonder. The soil of the prairies is extremely fertile and rich in organic matter. This is because the winters are cold and the summers are hot. These extremes of weather cause rapid evaporation and precipitation. Prairie soil has large quantities of nutrients, excellent structure, and good water-holding capacity.

The North American prairies correspond to the Pampas of Argentina, the Llanos in northern South America, the Steppes of Eurasia, and the High Veld of South Africa.

Because of the favorable climate and fertility of the soil, prairies are the wheat belts of their countries.

I.   Prairies

    A.   Description   D.   Prairies in Other Lands

        1.   1.

        2.   2.

    B.   Location   3.

        1.   4.

    C.   Characteristics of the Soil   E.   Principal Product

        1.   1.

        2.

        3.

        4.

COMPREHENSION   A. Outlining   1. *Takes notes effectively*

DIRECTIONS: Read the following selection and complete the outline form.

Desert Patrol

Exciting and romantic stories describe some policemen of the past: Texas Rangers breaking up lynch mobs just by coming on the scene, Canadian Mounties pursuing their men by canoe and dog sled, and, less well known but just as colorful, the members of the Desert Patrol of Jordan on their camels, finding travelers lost in the desert sands.

The scene today is changed and not very romantic. The Rangers have traded their horses for Chevys, the Mounties have traded their canoes and dog sleds for snowmobiles, and the Desert Patrol have traded their camels for jeeps and even helicopters.

In Jordan today, the Desert Patrol sometimes finds it more useful to use the Camel Corps in areas where Land Rovers would have difficulty. The day of the last patrol, however, is fast approaching.

The scarlet coats of the Royal Canadian Mounted Police—the Mounties—became the symbol of law, order, and safety for some 300,000 square miles of the wilderness of Canada. The khaki robes, blood-red belts, crossed cartridge belts, silver daggers, and red pistol cords of the Desert Patrol became the symbol of justice and help in the 25,000 square miles of desert that was their "beat." They won respect by rescuing lost tribesmen, bringing water to livestock, and settling arguments on the spot.

In the last few years, however, a very long drought has left a large area patrolled by the Desert Patrol bone dry. The wandering tribes have increasingly headed for the towns and cities. Not only have the wanderers fled, but those who still wander own jeeps and pickup trucks. The problems of these wanderers differ considerably from those of the camel drivers of the past.

I.   Desert Patrol

    A.   Policemen of the Past

        1.

        2.

        3.

    B.   Means of Transportation, Past and Present

        1.

        2.

    C.   Mounties and Desert Patrol Compared

        1.

        2.

        3.

    D.   Reasons for Changing Role of Desert Patrol

        1.

        2.

        3.

COMPREHENSION   A. Outlining   1. *Takes notes effectively*

DIRECTIONS: Read the following selection and complete the outline form.

Perfumes

Perfumes have been around for thousands of years. Egypt claims to have discovered the pleasure of fragrance, and the art of the perfumer goes back to as early as 2700 B.C.

Today, Egypt, more than any other country, can say that it perfumes the world. As much as 80 percent of natural jasmine products come from Egypt. Specialists in the art of perfume-making extract the sweet-smelling oils from countless flowers, leaves, roots, and herbs. These are exported to perfumers in Paris, London, New York, and Moscow.

Within sight of the well-known pyramids grow jasmine, roses, cassia, lemon-grass, geraniums, basil, and mint. North of Cairo grow carnations, surrounded by an unseen cloud of perfume. What is visible is a sea of green with, here and there, millions of tiny white stars, each bathed in the dew of the Nile.

Children harvest the jasmine. No taller than the jasmine bushes, they are trained for this very delicate work. They must use the thumb and forefinger as is done for picking cotton. The touch for jasmine must be skillful and delicate. Each blossom must be picked and placed in a basket individually.

It takes 880 pounds of jasmine to make about two pounds of pure jasmine wax. This means that one 11-pound can of jasmine exported to Paris uses 12.5 million blossoms.

I.   About Perfumes

    A.   Time and Place of Origin   D.   Flowers Grown and Location

        1.   1.

        2.   2.

    B.   Products Used in Production   E.   Harvest

        1.   1.

        2.   2.

        3.   3.

        4.

    C.   Where Exported

        1.

        2.

        3.

        4.

COMPREHENSION   A. Outlining   2. *Can sequence ideas or events*

DIRECTIONS: Read the following list of activities involved in planning a vacation. On the lines, write the number of the proper order in which these activities should take place.

_____ a.   Consider alternate routes, cost, and time.

_____ b.   Visit or contact a travel agent or read travel information.

_____ c.   Depart on time.

_____ d.   Decide on a place and length of stay.

_____ e.   Make a list of what to pack in your suitcase.

_____ f.   Check at your place of work for time and length of vacation.

_____ g.   Purchase traveler's checks.

_____ h.   Have a systematic vacation savings plan.

_____ i.   Purchase tickets, or get your car serviced if you are driving.

_____ j.   Reserve hotel or motel rooms.

_____ k.   Put the last items into the suitcase.

_____ l.   Decide on a method of transportation.

_____ m.   Pack your suitcase on the day before departure.

_____ n.   Select proper clothes for the place and season.

COMPREHENSION   A. Outlining   *2. Can sequence ideas or events*

DIRECTIONS: Read the following list of activities involved in writing a composition, essay, or term paper. Write the number of the proper order in which these activities should take place.

_____ a.   Make an outline.

_____ b.   List topics that appeal to you.

_____ c.   Set the work aside for a while.

_____ d.   Review a list of available topics.

_____ e.   Research the topic or subject chosen.

_____ f.   Type or write the final manuscript.

_____ g.   Reread what has been written.

_____ h.   Take notes on the subject.

_____ i.   Write the first draft.

_____ j.   Decide on a topic or subject.

_____ k.   Note the sources of notes for the bibliography.

_____ l.   Revise.

_____ m.   Revise a second time.

COMPREHENSION   A. Outlining   2. *Can sequence ideas or events*

DIRECTIONS: Read the following list of activities involved in doing your homework. On the lines, write the number of the proper order in which these activities should take place.

——— a.   Take home books, paper, whatever you will need.

——— b.   Make an outline.

——— c.   Prepare; put all you will need for the task on the desk or table.

——— d.   Listen very attentively in class.

——— e.   Turn off the radio or TV.

——— f.   Take notes in class.

——— g.   Hand in the homework.

——— h.   Check for errors; correct any mistakes.

——— i.   Be sure you understand exactly what the assignment is.

——— j.   Review the notes.

——— k.   Select your quiet study or work spot.

——— l.   Review what the task is.

——— m.   Work; write thoughtfully and carefully.

COMPREHENSION   A. Outlining   2. *Can sequence ideas or events*

DIRECTIONS: Read the following list of activities involved in planning a party. On the lines, write the number of the proper order in which you should perform these activities.

_____ a.   Prepare ahead of time what can be frozen or refrigerated.

_____ b.   Plan refreshments, food, and drink.

_____ c.   Plan the traffic pattern for the party room.

_____ d.   Purchase or make the refreshments.

_____ e.   Either write or phone invitations.

_____ f.   Prepare refreshments that need no refrigeration.

_____ g.   Decide on a date and time.

_____ h.   Put drinks on ice.

_____ i.   Select tapes or records and set them aside.

_____ j.   Decide on the number of people to invite, and who they will be.

_____ k.   Set the table or buffet.

_____ l.   Clean the rooms that will be used.

_____ m.   Decide to give a party.

_____ n.   Plan the entertainment: dancing, games, etc.

_____ o.   Greet the first guest.

_____ p.   Shower and dress.

_____ q.   Decide on the kind of party: formal, informal, masquerade, etc.

COMPREHENSION   A. Outlining   3. *Can skim for specific purposes*
                                 a. To locate facts and details

---

DIRECTIONS: You will be given a limited time to read the following selection. Then, list as many facts as you can remember from the reading.

War Means Refugees and Suffering

As the war in Zimbabwe-Rhodesia continues with increasing ferocity, more and more of the victims stream from the war zones into the towns. Many of these refugees have had their homes and possessions destroyed. They arrive with the clothes on their backs, clutching a few odds and ends they have managed to salvage from the horror they have left behind.

All buses to the capital of Salisbury, coming from all outlying areas, head first for Musika, a large bus stop and market at Harare. Many of the refugees get off at Harare with nowhere to go from there. Harare is therefore fast becoming a center for evicted and extremely poor people.

War refugees are not the only ones there. There is also a large number of town squatters, city dwellers who cannot find jobs in the war-torn country. They could not afford to live in a house even if they had the luck to find one. These poor people manage to survive by begging, making simple articles such as small brooms to sell, or simply rummaging around in rubbish dumps for something to eat or for something to sell. Musika has everything imaginable for sale.

Other squatters are at the Makabusi River near Harare. They consist mostly of foreigners from Mozambique who are stranded in Rhodesia because the borders of their homeland are closed. Living along the river is against the law. Peddling and begging are the way they manage to exist. Because their status is against the law, any shelter they try to set up is immediately torn down by the authorities.

Then there are the truly desperate people who have no place to stay. Like tramps, they sleep under the trees or on the porches of the shops at Musika. Whole families settle in the open. During the day they take their possessions with them as they move about.

Various organizations are trying to help with relief work or with resettlement programs. These include the Red Cross, World Vision, Christian Care, and the churches. The number of people to be helped never decreases; newcomers take the place of those who are resettled.

Facts remembered:

1.   6.

2.   7.

3.   8.

4.   9.

5.   10.

COMPREHENSION   A. Outlining   3. *Can skim for specific purposes*
                                   a. To locate facts and details

---

DIRECTIONS: You will be given a limited time to read the following selection. Then, list as many facts as you can remember from the reading.

Coming of Age

Just a few years ago, the United States celebrated its two-hundredth birthday. For a person, that would be old indeed. For a nation, however, it is only the coming of age.

All that has happened before can be compared to the childhood and adolescence of a person. During these stages, a person is not ordinarily very productive. The strength and energy of every day is needed to stay alive, to grow, and to develop. So it is with a young country; it is struggling to survive and to grow. Little time is left to write about the struggle. It is recorded, however, in the minds of those who live through those days and who later relate their experiences to their children. It is recorded in the kinds of buildings they put up, first primitive shelter and later designed for greater comfort. It is recorded in the articles made and used, whether in homes, farms, schools, churches, stores, or for transportation on land or over water. It is also recorded in letters and in account books kept by conscientious merchants.

Many people tend to throw away what is old and used. Fortunately, there are hoarders who cannot bear to part with anything. Thanks to them, we have today the very tools, kitchen utensils, furniture, pictures, and books that were the prized possessions of our ancestors during the childhood of our country.

Some of these objects are carefully preserved and displayed in museums. Others are found in restored villages like Sturbridge in Massachusetts, or Williamsburg in Virginia. Still others are scattered among the numberless antique shops that are found everywhere. Attics have been explored and emptied. One person's junk will become the proud possession of another.

America, now a youth come of age and realizing the historical importance of these objects, hungrily searches for these relics of the past, buying them up to preserve them for still further generations.

Facts remembered:

1.

2.

    a.   d.

    b.   e.

    c.   f.

COMPREHENSION   **A. Outlining**   **3.** *Can skim for specific purposes*
                                              a. To locate facts and details

DIRECTIONS: Read this selection. Then answer the questions about facts and details in the selection.

A By-Product of Road Building

During the 1950s and since, all over these vast United States a gigantic road-building program was undertaken. It was the heyday of the automobile. Roads were needed to facilitate their easy and speedy access to cities and to increase the speed of travel between cities. Two-lane, crown-top tar roads disappeared and, as if by magic, became four- and six-lane super highways with overpasses, underpasses, and access roads. Miles and miles of fields and woods were transformed.

Roads were also needed in the cities. Engineers wanted the most direct routes. Buildings were vacated and then destroyed to make room for the highways, beltways, or parkways. At first, there was hardly any resistance. Roads were needed. It was that simple. Their construction provided jobs. It was progress! And it all happened very fast.

Then, resistance flared up. People wanted roads and jobs and progress. They did not, however, want destruction. Sometimes buildings, even sections of cities, that had historical and architectural value were scheduled to be torn down. Protests began on a small scale at first, often by a group of women pushing baby carriages and refusing to give way to a bulldozer. Later protests became more sophisticated and better organized. Demands were made to see plans and drawings before the bulldozers arrived. Alternate routes were suggested that would be just as efficient but not as destructive. The people were heard and changes were made.

This awakened other people to the existence of buildings that were beautiful in design, in proportions and in materials. They could not be duplicated because of the higher costs of labor and materials. People also took notice of sections of cities once held in high regard but now timeworn and dilapidated, sometimes abandoned. Many of these neighborhoods were right in the heart of the cities. The battle to save them had been won but the spoils of victory were eyesores. They presented a new challenge to American ingenuity, shrewdness, and know-how. The challenge was taken up.

1. Why were better roads needed? _____

2. Why was there no resistance in the cities at the outset? _____

3. How were the first protests carried out? _____

4. What demands were made? _____

5. What resulted from the demands? _____

6. Why could buildings not be duplicated? _____

7. What new challenge resulted? _____

                                                               VI

COMPREHENSION   A. Outlining   3. *Can skim for specific purposes*
                                 a. To locate facts and details

DIRECTIONS: Briefly outline ten facts and/or details you learn from reading the following selection.

Viscount Ferdinand Marie de Lesseps

De Lesseps is a name associated with two great canals, the Suez Canal and the Panama Canal.

The viscount, whose life spanned the nineteenth century, was born in 1805 and died in 1894. He was an engineer and a diplomat. He began his diplomatic service for France as a consul in 1825. Later, he served as minister to Spain.

Still later, while he was a diplomat in Egypt, de Lesseps got the idea for a Suez Canal. In 1854, he obtained from the viceroy of Egypt the necessary permission to open a passage through the Isthmus of Suez. He played an important part in organizing the Suez Canal Company and succeeded in raising more than half the capital needed from subscriptions from French citizens. From 1859 to 1869, he supervised the actual construction and became known all over the world when his venture proved successful.

In 1878, de Lesseps became president of a French company that was formed to construct the Panama Canal. Work was begun in 1881. The success of the Suez Canal was not to be repeated. Poor planning, disease among the workers, construction troubles, and not enough money caused the company to go bankrupt in 1889. De Lesseps was brought to trial for corruption and mismanagement. Although sentenced to prison, he did not serve. Observers then and since believed de Lesseps was guilty only of negligence.

French courts in 1894 transferred the rights and assets to a new company. It was these rights that were later purchased by the United States.

Facts remembered:

1.   6.

2.   7.

3.   8.

4.   9.

5.   10.

COMPREHENSION   A. Outlining   **3. *Can skim for specific purposes***
  b. To select and reject materials to fit a
    certain purpose

DIRECTIONS: Read the following selection and then fill out the form below.

Your Own Time

You enter school in September and immediately start the countdown of days to the next summer vacation. Is it that you don't like school? Not necessarily. Even if you liked it, would you dare admit it? But you don't ever hesitate to say you can't wait for the long summer break. And why not? That's when you don't have to get up at a certain time, get dressed, eat breakfast, or catch the bus, ride the bicycle, or walk to school to be there on time. Because you don't have to, the day becomes inviting and you often get up before you're called. You don't have to have reading at a certain hour, followed by math, followed by gym. So it's fun to pick up a paperback or magazine, find a cool and shady corner, and read for hours. You don't have to do the exercises or play the game the teacher has selected; you can choose. You run or swim or ride your bicycle until you're exhausted. You don't have to pack your lunch to take to school so you ask for the same peanut butter and jelly sandwich you complained about all year.

Summer vacation is your own time for your own decisions.

A.   Things you don't have to do:

  1.   4.

  2.   5.

  3.

B.   Things that become fun include:

  1.

  2.

  3.

  4.

COMPREHENSION   A. Outlining   3. *Can skim for specific purposes*
                                      b. To select and reject materials to fit a
                                      certain purpose

DIRECTIONS: Read the following selection and then fill out the form below.

Sails

The combined talents of an oilman-sailor and a sixth generation sail-maker may well bring back the sight of sails on the high seas. In an experiment in the summer of 1980, two 800-horsepower tugs towed an oil drilling rig from Galveston, Texas, to Halifax, Nova Scotia. The rig was 247 feet long by 200 feet wide, with three towers 410 feet high. There is nothing unusual about that as rigs go. But this one also had two sails 75 feet across the base and 180 feet high. The 2500 nautical miles were covered in sixteen days, approximately one day less than the usual time for such an undertaking.

By harnessing the wind, the sails increased the speed of the rig that was being towed. They also reduced the roll of the rig; this in turn decreased the drag on the tugs. Since the workload of the tugs was cut down, so was their use of fuel. Time was saved, fuel was saved, and so were hundreds of thousands of dollars.

The men who developed this system foresee its application to other tugs, to coastal freighters, and even to ocean-going vessels. With a combination of the old and the modern, there will be sails on the seas again!

Use of sails on the rigs resulted in:

1.   5.

2.   6.

3.   7.

4.

Experience with the sails may be applied to:

1.

2.

3.

COMPREHENSION   **A. Outlining**   **3. *Can skim for specific purposes***
b. To select and reject materials to fit a
certain purpose

DIRECTIONS: Read the following selection and then fill out the form below.

Wine Making

California is considered tops among the wine-making states in producing premium wines. Some authorities are forecasting that this position will be challenged in the near future by the oldest wine region in the United States, the Hudson River Valley in New York.

Several factors are responsible for this possible threat. Old vineyards are being brought back to life by a new breed of owners. Some of these new vineyard owners decided not to use the native Concord and Niagara grapes. Instead, they planted French-American hybrids which had been developed by a Maryland man who crossed the best French vines and native American varieties. Others turned to European vines cultivated to withstand the harsh and cold New York winter. These European hybrid grapes did especially well because of the angle of the slopes, the kind of soil, and the effect which the Hudson River has on the climate of the valley.

Nature alone is not responsible for raising the hopes of New York's small vineyard owners. The state legislature helped by passing laws favoring them. One law reduces the annual license fee; another permits small vineyard owners to sell a good part of their wine directly from the winery; still a third law exempts grape trellis materials from state sales taxes.

So, vineyards are part of the scenery of the Hudson Valley once again, and the high quality of the table wines produced there could be a threat to other wine-making areas.

Factors contributing to the development of Hudson Valley wineries:

1.   5.

2.   6.

3.   7.

4.

COMPREHENSION   A. Outlining   *3. Can skim for specific purposes*
     b. To select and reject materials to fit a
     certain purpose

DIRECTIONS: Read the following selection and then fill out the form below.

Self-Discipline

"Discipline" has so many meanings. To a student, it means the order maintained in the classroom, in the building, or on the bus. To a soldier, it means drills, marches, bivouacs, polished shoes, cleaned and pressed uniform, squared shoulders, or pride in his or her outfit. One could go on and on with examples. No discipline, however, whether it is school, military, religious, or professional, is possible without its most important ingredient of self-discipline.

Self-discipline results from training yourself to do what has to be done promptly and well. It means listening to the small voice within you that says "You ought to," and pushing away the temptation to take things easy, to dawdle along, to put off until later, to try to get away with doing nothing or as little as possible.

Even a casual look at the people we admire, those who are successful in what they do, reveals that they all have something in common. Their profession or career has a body of information, of training, of demands, to which they have committed themselves for many hours daily for prolonged periods. In doing so, they keep on choosing hard work, persistence, long hours, and sometimes disappointment and tears. But they stay with it. Very rare is the success story without those elements of giving of oneself and of sacrificing something. Think of the hours when the no-hit pitcher practices those throws; of the conditioning a boxer goes through for months before he enters the ring; of all the scales, exercises, and lessons the musician goes through every day for years; of the long hours and years required to become a doctor and the additional hours and years needed to become a surgeon. No masterpiece of art was ever the first attempt of any artist. No productive life just happens. No marathon runner runs the 26 miles the first time.

It all starts with denying yourself the easy way, the soft way, choosing instead and practicing day after day the hard and the difficult until it becomes second nature. The self-disciplined person is a strong person. The self-disciplined person is a productive, useful, and successful person.

Self discipline comes from: Examples of self-disciplined persons:

1.   1.

2.   2.

3.   3.

4.   4.

It results in: 5.

1.   6.

2.

3.

4.

COMPREHENSION   A. Outlining   *4. Can identify main ideas of paragraphs*

DIRECTIONS: Read the following paragraphs. Write the main idea of each paragraph on the line beneath it.

Bridges

Bridges are everywhere and they are of many kinds. They all share the same purpose, which is to permit people on foot or in vehicles to go from one point to another over water, through an obstacle, or across a large, deep space.

1. _____

Even in very ancient times, primitive people solved the problem of getting to the other side of an obstacle. They would throw a log across a stream. Some would take two vines or weave ropes of fibers and throw them across the obstacle to be bridged. One vine or rope served as a handhold, the other as a footwalk.

2. _____

Traces of bridges built between 4000 and 2000 B.C. have been found. They give evidence that stone and bricks were used to build arched bridges. Many such arched bridges, built by the Romans, are still standing.

3. _____

In the early history of the United States, wood, the most abundant and cheapest material, was used to build bridges. It did not, however, lend itself to arched bridges. Because rot or fire can destroy wood, it is very seldom used for bridges any more.

4. _____

In the middle of the nineteenth century, cast iron and wrought iron were used in building bridges. The Victoria Bridge over the Saint Lawrence River at Montreal in Canada is an example of such a bridge. Cast iron, however, has a low resistance to longitudinal stress.

5. _____

When the process of converting cast iron into steel was discovered, bridge building was revolutionized. Gradually, longer and longer bridges have been able to be built because of the flexibility of steel.

6. _____

COMPREHENSION   **A. Outlining**   *4. Can identify main ideas of paragraphs*

DIRECTIONS: Read the following paragraphs. Write the main idea of each paragraph on the line beneath it.

Calendars

Just what is a calendar? Days, weeks, months, numbers? A calendar is a system of reckoning time with reference to the beginning, length, and divisions of the year.

1. _____

Natural and ordinary events, such as the cycle of the sun through the seasons and the recurrent phases of the moon, are easy to observe and note. Records of these observations form the basis of calendars.

2. _____

Some people have reckoned time by the sun and some by the moon. The earth's orbit around the sun takes 365 days, 5 hours, 48 minutes, and 46 seconds. This constitutes the solar year. The moon goes through its phases in about 29½ days. The result is that the lunar year comes to more than 354 days, 8 hours, and 48 minutes. Since very early days, this has caused a problem in reconciling and harmonizing solar and lunar reckonings.

3. _____

Months and years cannot be divided exactly into days. Years cannot be easily divided into months. As skill in calculating developed, prevailing systems came to depend upon a combination of the solar and the lunar years. A device called "intercalation" was developed. Intercalation is inserting an extra day or an extra month into the yearly calendar.

4. _____

Practical people felt that reckoning of the days and years was necessary to determine sacred days, to plan for the future, and to keep a record of the past.

5. _____

COMPREHENSION   A. Outlining   *4. Can identify main ideas of paragraphs*

DIRECTIONS: Read the following paragraphs. Write the main idea of each paragraph on the line beneath it.

Reading

Just what is reading anyway? One definition states that it is the process by which the mind interprets symbols. These symbols may be letters, numbers, or even pictures. Assembled in different arrangements, they convey ideas.

1. _____

Before the invention of the printing press by Gutenberg around 1450, the ability to read was not considered important for most people. Reading was seen as the special expertise of the clergy and certain members of the nobility.

2. _____

Since that time, more and more was gradually put into print. Today, everything that is known is in print in one form or another. Laws, directions, tax forms, job application forms, the news, history, fiction, communication; all use print. As a result, reading is not only essential for all, but it is vital.

3. _____

The inability to read is called illiteracy. Laws requiring childhood education have fought the battle against illiteracy by providing instruction. Most citizens of advanced nations can read. Where illiteracy is due to poor vision, faulty eye movements, personal handicaps, or poor teaching, great efforts are being made and great amounts of money are being spent to make up for the deficiencies. The ability to read is considered of highest importance.

4. _____

COMPREHENSION   A. Outlining   4. *Can identify main ideas of paragraphs*

DIRECTIONS: Read the following paragraphs. Write the main idea of each paragraph on the line beneath it.

Rock Music

The type of music that has been popular in the United States and elsewhere since 1954 is called rock music. It is a combination of several American music styles. These include black guitar-accompanied blues; black rhythm and blues with saxophone solos; black and white gospel music; white country and western music; and the songs of white popular crooners and harmony groups.

1. _____

When it first appeared, rock music was called "rock-and-roll," until 1964 when it began to be called "rock music." While there was a continuing relationship with what had gone before, there was also a break with the past. The influence of the Beatles from 1962 on and that of Bob Dylan from 1965 were largely responsible for the change.

2. _____

A 1955 record by Bill Haley and the Comets, "Rock Around the Clock," was the first rock-and-roll record to sell in the millions. This music appealed to youth because it had an exciting off beat and its lyrics gave an urgent call to dance and action. It also put black rhythm and blues into a music form that adolescent white audiences could understand.

3. _____

Rock-and-roll was for and about adolescents. Its lyrics were about the teenage life style and its problems: school, cars, summer vacation, parents, and first love. The heavy beat, loudness, lyrics, and raving delivery gave teenagers a feeling that they were defying adult authority.

4. _____

COMPREHENSION   **A. Outlining**   ***5. Can interpret characters' feelings***

DIRECTIONS: Follow the directions after each selection.

A.

It was the morning after Halloween. Joe had been in his usual cheerful, bouncy mood when he rose and while he bathed and shaved. He came to the breakfast table whistling. He was still gaily doing so as he strode out to his car, which was parked in its usual spot next to the garage. Joe stopped in the middle of a whistled note. There was the pride and glory of his youthful life—his TR7—with every tire flat and every window soaped up! In no time, joviality gave way to anger. How could they do this to his pride and joy?

Fill in the blanks.

1. Joe appears to be a _____ morning person.

2. His car gave him a feeling of _____ .

3. Halloween pranksters made Joe very _____ .

B.

Grandma sat down in the recliner and jerked it so that the footrest came up to meet her tired legs and feet. A long, deep sigh came from her and then a smile appeared on her face. She was reliving the whole day: the arrival of the children, the hugs of the grandchildren, the teasing and laughing around the dinner table, everyone pitching in to help clean up, and the games they all played afterward. Yes, it had indeed been a Thanksgiving Day to remember.

Cross out the feelings that do not apply: contentment—regret—satisfaction—worry—gratitude—affection—tiredness—pride—resentment—joy

C.

The telephone rang. Louise, who had been up and down from her chair a dozen times in the past half-hour, almost tripped getting to the phone. "Hello?" her voice quavered. "Is this 239-6980?" a strange voice asked. Louise's heart skipped a beat. "No, I'm sorry, it isn't," she managed to answer. "Sorry, ma'am," the telephone voice apologized and the phone was still. Slowly, looking at the instrument in her hands, she put it down. She was trembling. Her hands were clammy. Where were the twins? Why weren't they home yet? What had happened?

List as many of Louise's feelings as you can.

COMPREHENSION   A. Outlining   *5. Can interpret characters' feelings*

DIRECTIONS: Follow the directions after each selection.

A.

Marie walked gracefully, straight and tall. A lingering smile on her lips repeatedly broadened as she wished a good morning to all she met on her walk to the office. "Pardon me," she said to a young boy on a skateboard who came close to knocking her down. The momentary fright had challenged her smile, but it returned. The morning was bright and sunny yet pleasantly cool. Another promising day! How wonderful it was to be alive! Such were her thoughts.

Cross out the words that do not describe Marie's feelings: Marie was an optimistic, self-centered, considerate, rude, cheerful, outgoing, insensitive, grateful-to-be-alive, unappreciative young lady.

B.

Paul was sitting alone and reading in the living room of the huge Munchin house. He had volunteered to housesit while the owners, his friends, were away. His main task was to keep the house looking occupied. He was glad he had volunteered his services. He felt he owed it to his friends, who were worried about the thefts that had been reported recently in the neighborhood. Being there for them was almost as good as being with them, although nothing could really replace that. He got up and went through the house once more, checking windows and doors, putting out some lights, and turning others on. He returned to the living room.

Cross out the descriptions that do not apply: Paul was a grateful, spiteful, thoughtful, irresponsible, considerate, reliable, reckless, loving friend.

C.

Jimmy stirred and opened his eyes. In the semidarkness, his surroundings seemed unfamiliar. His heartbeat quickened. Where was he? What was that large, black shape on the right? Was it moving? Maybe if he closed his eyes to open them again, he'd know where he was. He dared not move. He heard breathing, held his breath, and realized it was himself he had heard. He peeked with one eye. Shadows were moving; everything looked weird. He opened the other eye, stared hard, and made himself look around. He relaxed. The moon was like a spotlight behind the big tree by his window and the summer breeze was making the limbs dance on his walls. He was safe in his own bed. He sighed, turned over, and was soon asleep again.

List the feelings Jimmy experienced in the order in which they are described:

COMPREHENSION   A. Outlining   *5. Can interpret characters' feelings*

DIRECTIONS: Follow the directions after each selection.

A.

A car stopped. A broad-shouldered, short, blond youth got out from the driver's side and half ran to the passenger's side. He opened the door and, with great care, bowed and smiled as he helped the aging woman to get out. When she had straightened up, he said, "Easy, now, Nana," giving her his arm. "Easy. No hurry. That's it. Just a few more steps. Lean on me, Nana. It's kind of uphill." When they reached the door, a tall, thin young woman was holding it open. "Here's my favorite girlfriend, Mom," he said. "Take care of her, now. She's precious, only one of a kind!"

Answer the questions briefly:

1. What kind of youth is described?

   _____

2. What are his feelings for his grandmother?

   _____

B.

It had been a long day but a good one. The father and his teenaged son had gotten a lot done. After an early but hearty breakfast, they had mowed the lawn, with the son running the mower and the father trimming the edges along the walks. When they had finished, they lunched on sandwiches and milk, and then drove to Grandma and Grandpa's house, five miles away. There they did the same tasks over again. True, the yard wasn't as big, but the grass was taller because during their absence it had been neglected. It was more difficult to cut and took longer. In addition, the privet hedge had to be trimmed. They worked side by side, talking about this and that, joking and teasing each other, happy to be together. When they were finished, they put away their tools and drove back home. Afterward, when dinner was over, they sat chatting. They were tired after their long, hard work, but it was a pleasant tiredness. They felt ...

Complete the story by writing how they felt. Give reasons for their feelings.

COMPREHENSION A. Outlining 5. *Can interpret characters' feelings*

DIRECTIONS: Follow the directions after each selection.

A.

Greg came home from high school football practice and didn't seem quite as exhausted as usual. He appeared to be having trouble with his face. His mother looked at him, wondering. She knew his love of football and she attended all of his games. He had been elected captain; he always played his heart out. His team had won last Saturday's game largely because of Greg's leadership and tenacity. But the season overall had been disappointing. She knew he was holding back something and again wondered what it might be. Suddenly, Greg let a big, broad smile get the best of his face as he looked at his mother. Relieved, she asked, "Good news?" Right at that moment, Andy, Greg's brother, came bursting into the house, breathless from running, yelling, "Hey, Ma! Guess what? Greg was named most valuable player of the week!"

1. Describe Greg's feelings.

_____

2. Describe his mother's feelings.

_____

3. What kind of a person is Greg?

_____

B.

The mail was usually on the hall table by noon. Today it was almost one o'clock and the table was bare. The letter Joan was expecting had been promised for today. Her heart sank. That must surely mean she was not going to receive the scholarship. Without it, she would have to give up hopes of going to college. Disappointment began to take hold of her but she battled it, refusing to give in. Well, she would get a job and earn the money, even if it meant postponing college. But to college she would go! She would get there, she vowed.

The feelings Joan experiences, one after the other, are:

COMPREHENSION   A. Outlining   *6. Can identify topic sentences*

DIRECTIONS: Read each paragraph and write the topic sentence below it.

1. Seasoning with herbs and spices is no mystery. Cooking with them is just as simple as using salt and pepper. There are no hard and fast rules. When you use herbs, you can apply the much laughed at expression, "a pinch of this and a pinch of that." Suiting your taste is the best guide to follow.

   _____

2. The classic shirtdress may be worn everywhere. Its very name requires that it have a front opening like a shirt. It can be made in different styles by changing the lines of the yoke. The skirt can be wide and swirling or narrow and slit. Sleeves can be short or long.

   _____

3. The education of 45 million young Americans is a very important matter. What will their education be like in 2018? It is too soon to know, but it is not too early to wonder about it.

   _____

4. The essential needs of children must be met. Throughout the world there are millions of children whose most basic needs are not met because of poverty and ignorance. UNICEF assists a variety of programs in health care, nutrition, and education to meet requirements for the very lives of girls and boys in over 100 Asian, African, and Latin American countries.

   _____

COMPREHENSION   A. Outlining   6. *Can identify topic sentences*

DIRECTIONS: Read each paragraph and write the topic sentence below it.

1. Unusual quiet prevailed that morning. There was no sound of automobiles or buses taking people to work. The voices of children walking to school were noticeably absent. The stillness was eerie. It was Friday. Then she remembered. It was a holiday.

2. Some herbs enhance the flavor of certain foods more than others. Sage, for instance, has an affinity for pork dishes, savory for beef, marjoram for lamb, and basil for tomato. Experience has taught us that these combinations are successful.

3. Our new gift catalog contains over 200 items, allowing the buyer to choose just the right gift for everyone on his or her giving list or for home entertaining. Everything from "soup to nuts" is available, and our company pledge of quality and service applies to all of our products.

4. There had been no rain to speak of for weeks. The days were sunny and warm, the skies were a bright blue, and lawns were brown. Farmers saw their crops drying in the fields before they could ripen. The Farmer's Almanac had been right again. It had predicted a mild winter, a wet spring, a hot summer, and drought in the fall.

COMPREHENSION   A. Outlining   *6. Can identify topic sentences*

DIRECTIONS: Read each paragraph and write the topic sentence below it.

1. In the world of women's fashions, a classic is a dress that is suitable for wearing everywhere and forever. Such a fashion is the shirtdress, sometimes also called a shirtwaist dress. It is so called because it has a bodice and a front opening tailored like those of a dress shirt.

_____

2. Sooner or later, we all begin to wish for change. While there are some things that must retain permanence, there are many others that can fill the need we all have. Sometimes just rearranging the furniture satisfies this need. A new set of curtains or drapes, a fresh new lamp shade, and a different color scheme are all suggestions that a home decorator would make to fulfill the wish for change.

_____

3. "Eclectic" is a nice, accommodating word. It could be called a fence-sitting word. If your taste in art is not modern art, nor impressionism, nor classicism, but certain masterpieces from each school, your taste in art is eclectic. If you like back-to-basics in education but you also like and use some of the newest ideas, you are eclectic. Being eclectic means not following any one system but selecting and using what are considered the best elements of all systems.

_____

4. New Federal Communications Commission proposals would put hundreds, possibly thousands, of new television stations on the air. The proposals are intended to increase many different kinds of programming throughout the nation. Involved is a new type of television service that uses so-called translators as mini TV stations. Unlike present stations, their telecasting range would be limited to a radius of approximately ten miles.

_____

COMPREHENSION   A. Outlining   6. *Can identify topic sentences*

DIRECTIONS: Read each paragraph and write the topic sentence below it.

1. In the history of science, not infrequently a creative leap forward is made. Someone has learned all that could be learned and read every word written about a particular thing. The scientist lets all that simmer in his or her mind for a while. Then, sometimes slowly, sometimes suddenly, the simmering yields ideas and concepts that just feel right; they make good sense but there just isn't any evidence to support them. So the scientist sets about to look for the evidence and the proof.

_____

2. Where we live contributes much to what we are. The people of Maine have a vast knowledge of the sea and of the immense woodlands that are theirs. In New Hampshire, the very short coastline and the awesome silent mountains make for a particular breed of person. The lives of Kansas people are closely related to the sun and the rain which influence their farming. The deserts of Arizona are sought by its people for their life-restoring dryness.

_____

3. Zoos have changed. Years ago, going to the zoo generally meant promenading past large outdoor areas enclosed by high wire fences. In a specific area would be found the long-necked giraffe; next to that might be caves with bears and their neighbors, the elephants. It was fun and interesting because it was strange. A trip to the zoo today means riding in a train-like vehicle that wanders through a jungle setting. You sit and watch closely because you never know what animal you'll be seeing next. Now they are not enclosed separately but in settings that are more like their natural habitats.

_____

4. Size is often not important in choosing a dog. Training is. A twenty-pound, untrained, unspoiled dog will be much more difficult to handle, let alone train, than a well-mannered large dog.

_____

COMPREHENSION   B. Following Directions

DIRECTIONS: You are sending a package containing three things to a friend or relative in a foreign country—Canada, Mexico, Haiti, Italy, Thailand, India, etc. The post office clerk gives you the form below to fill in. Don't panic. Take your time, read it carefully, and then fill it in.

THIS LABEL FOR INTERNATIONAL PARCEL POST USE. COMPLETE AND APPLY ON ADDRESS SIDE OF PARCEL. BEND AT SLIT AND PEEL OFF BACKING	**PARCEL POST CUSTOMS DECLARATION — UNITED STATES OF AMERICA**		

PARCEL POST CUSTOMS DECLARATION — UNITED STATES OF AMERICA

INSTRUCTIONS GIVEN BY SENDER *Dispositions de l'Expéditeur*	QTY	USE INK OR TYPEWRITER ITEMIZED LIST OF CONTENTS	VALUE (U.S. $)
If undeliverable as addressed: *Au cas de non-livraison:* ☐ **Return to sender. Return charges guaranteed.** *Le colis doit être renvoyé à l'expéditeur,* *qui s'engage à payer les frais de retour.* ☐ Forward to. (*Le colis doit être réexpé-* *dié à*):			
☐ Abandon. (*Abandon du colis.*)			
(Sender's Signature—*Signature de l'expediteur*) NOTE: Your signature affirms that your item does not contain any dangerous article prohibited by postal regulations.			
MAILING OFFICE DATE STAMP	LBS.		
	OZS.		
	POSTAGE $	ACCEPTING CLERK'S INITIALS	INSURED VALUE (U.S. $)

PS Form 2966-A, Aug. 1979

COMPREHENSION   B. Following Directions

DIRECTIONS: Read carefully and fill out the census form below. Be as factual as possible. You may make up information about which you are not sure. Be sure to follow directions exactly!

PLEASE PRINT OR WRITE CLEARLY

- I have checked with the members of my household, and I believe that one (or more) of us was NOT counted in the 1990 Census.

- On April 1, 1990, I lived at

_____ (House number) _____ (Street, road, etc.) _____ (Apartment number or location)

_____ (City) _____ (State) _____ (ZIP code)

- This address is located between

_____ (Street, road, etc.)   and   _____ (Street, road, etc.)

_____ (County)

- I am listing below the name and required information for myself and each member of my household.

INSTRUCTIONS FOR WHOM TO INCLUDE IN YOUR HOUSEHOLD: APRIL 1, 1990

PLEASE INCLUDE

All family members and other relatives living here, including babies.

All lodgers, boarders, and other persons living here.

All persons who usually live here but are temporarily away.

All persons with a home elsewhere but who stay here most of the week while working or attending college.

Anyone staying or visiting here who had no other home.

DO NOT INCLUDE

Any college student who stays somewhere else while attending college.

Any person away from here in the Armed Forces or in an institution such as a home for the aged or mental hospital.

Any person who usually stays somewhere else most of the week while working there.

Any person visiting here who has a usual home elsewhere.

NAMES OF ALL PERSONS LIVING IN THIS HOUSEHOLD ON APRIL 1, 1990 AND THOSE STAYING OR VISITING HERE WHO HAD NO OTHER HOME

Please list on Line (1) a household member who owns or rents the home.

Last name	First name	Middle initial	How is this person related to the person on line 1? For example: Husband/wife Son/daughter Father/mother Grandson Mother-in-law Roomer, boarder Partner, roommate	Is this person — Male or Female M or F	Is this person — White Black (Negro) Japanese Chinese Filipino Korean Vietnamese Indian (Amer.) Print tribe	Asian Indian Hawaiian Guamanian Samoan Eskimo Aleut Other — Specify	When was this person born? Month / Year	Is this person — Now married Widowed Divorced Separated Single (never married)	Is this person of Spanish/Hispanic origin or descent? No – Not Spanish/Hispanic Yes – Mexican Mexican–American Chicano Puerto Rican Cuban Other Spanish/Hispanic
①									
②									
③									
④									
⑤									
⑥									

(If there are more than 6 persons, use an additional sheet)

- Name of person who filled this form

TELEPHONE NUMBER:

Form Approved: O.M.B. No. 41-S78006

U.S. DEPARTMENT OF COMMERCE BUREAU OF THE CENSUS FORM D-25

NOTICE — This census is authorized by title 13, United States Code, and you are required by law to answer the questions to the best of your knowledge. The same law protects the confidentiality of your answers. Census employees are subject to fine and/or imprisonment for any disclosure of your answers. Only after 72 years does your information become available to other government agencies or the public.

Cut along dotted line

GPO 964-634

COMPREHENSION   **B. Following Directions**

DIRECTIONS: You want to apply for a charge account at a local department store. You are given the application form below. Read it very carefully and then fill it in. Make up facts if necessary.

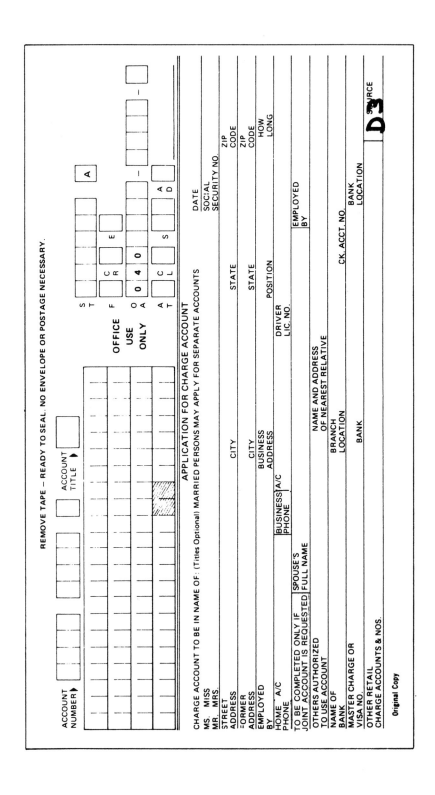

COMPREHENSION   B. Following Directions

DIRECTIONS: Read the application below very carefully. Fill it out for only one of the purposes for which it is intended. Be sure you do everything required. Where identification is requested, indicate what you will offer.

BIRTH OR DEATH CERTIFICATE

DATE OF BIRTH: _____ _____

DATE OF DEATH: _____

NAME: _____

FATHER'S NAME: _____

MOTHER'S MAIDEN NAME:_____

PURPOSE FOR WHICH THE CERTIFICATE IS TO BE USED. PLEASE CHECK ONE:

PASSPORT: _____   SOCIAL SERVICES: _____

DISABILITY: _____   MILITARY: _____

LEGAL PURPOSES: _____   IDENTIFICATION: _____

SCHOOL: _____   INSURANCE: _____

DRIVER'S LICENSE: _____   OTHER, SPECIFY: _____

THE APPLICANT MUST BE *18 YEARS OF AGE* IN ORDER TO OBTAIN SAID CERTIFICATE.
PROPER IDENTIFICATION IS NECESSARY.
THE FEE FOR SAID CERTIFICATE IS $2.00 PER CERTIFICATE.
PLEASE MAKE CHECK OR MONEY ORDER OUT TO THE VILLAGE OF:

_____

SIGNATURE OF APPLICANT: _____

ADDRESS: _____

CITY: _____

COMPREHENSION   C. Drawing Conclusions

DIRECTIONS: Read each selection. Then, answer the question following it after reaching a conclusion from the text.

1. Crowds lined the streets. People had begun to arrive about an hour ago and they were still coming. Traffic in the street had diminished gradually until only a police car drove slowly by, returning just as slowly afterward. Balloon venders were doing a brisk business on street corners. Side streets were barricaded. An air of expectancy was conveyed by ears straining to detect the first notes or the first beat that would herald the approach of the spectacle all had come to see.

    Why were people lining the streets and why had all traffic stopped?

2. Grandpa was sitting on the edge of the front seat. His daughters had never seen him so excited. He was giving directions. "Turn here. Now, go right. Drive more slowly. It's changed," he said, "but I know where I am!" Suddenly he shouted, "Stop!" Very quickly for a man his age, he got out of the car, went up the walk to the door of a house, and knocked. Soon, his daughters observed him speaking to someone in the doorway. A person came out, reached out, and embraced Grandpa. When they both turned and started walking toward the car, the resemblance between them was startling.

    Where had Grandpa directed his daughters?

3. Peter and Paul entered the room with apprehension. A woman in a white uniform came out to greet them. Recognizing them, she said, "Great! You're ahead of time. We'll take you right away." The boys looked around. One wall had a poster promoting the use of floss. On a filing cabinet was a huge pair of dentures.

    Where are the boys?

COMPREHENSION   C. Drawing Conclusions

DIRECTIONS: Read each selection. Then, answer the question following it after drawing a conclusion from the text.

1. Along the course she was traveling, the scenery kept shifting rapidly. There were wide open spaces of fields. Scattered here and there were houses, some small, some old. There were woods. There were tunnels that turned day into night. Soon, small villages gave way to buildings that seemed to get taller and closer together. Then there was a final tunnel, a very long one. The speed decreased gradually until they finally stopped. A voice over the loudspeaker cried out, "Grand City Station! All passengers out!"

    How was she traveling?

2. Daisy kept insisting that her friend Molly come to visit her. Molly couldn't for a hundred reasons. Half-crying, half-laughing, she finally promised Daisy she would come for a visit when banana trees grew pears.

    When will Molly visit Daisy?

3. David and John were excited. The plane was headed west, taking them to visit their older married brother. That was excitement enough but they were also going to see the Golden Gate Bridge. They were going to be able to ride the cable cars and visit Chinatown and Fisherman's Wharf! Maybe they'd even see the redwood forest. Remembering a movie they had seen, John said, "I sure hope there won't be an earthquake!"

    Where were David and John going?

4. Excitement pervaded the town. It was celebrating its 375th birthday. Many of its children, who had risen to positions of power and prestige, whose achievements in the sciences, business, art, and education had given the town fame, were expected. Practically every family had visitors. Hotels and motels for miles around were fully booked. People were heading for the new mall to hear the speeches. There were flags, balloons, and bunting everywhere. It was the speaker's stand with the great seal of the United States that introduced their most famous son and principal speaker even before his arrival attended by a horde of Secret Service men.

    Who is to be the principal guest?

COMPREHENSION   C. Drawing Conclusions

DIRECTIONS: Read each selection. Then, answer the question following it after drawing a conclusion from the text.

1. The applause died down. The speaker continued, encouraged. He was making promises now, promises about reducing taxes, providing jobs, doing better than his opponent ever could do. All they had to do was vote for him.

    Who was making a speech?

_____

2. "We love that guy," the boys were telling their parents. "He's strict but he's fair. He makes us work hard but he doesn't give assignments over holidays and not often over weekends. When he has finished explaining something, you've understood it. And if you ask questions, he doesn't get mad. He's the greatest!"

    Who are the boys talking about?

_____

3. Ruth was very late getting home. Her face was red. She emptied her tote bag and its contents on the laundry room floor. Along with her swimsuit and towel, sand fell out.

    Where had Ruth been?

_____

4. Waking up, Barbara looked slowly about her. Everything was out of place. The dresser should be over there on the right where the door was and the door should be on the left of the bed. Instead, there was a window. Strange! Her room had two windows. She looked hard at the window. Instead of the familiar oak tree, what greeted her eyes were rooftops, endless rooftops. She remained as if suspended for a moment. Then she smiled. Of course, she wasn't at home!

    Where was Barbara?

_____

5. Day was ending. The sun had retired, trailing behind it a sky that was undecided about what color to wear, changing from gold to purple. Everything was still clearly visible. Night had still not claimed its reign.

    What time of day is it?

_____

COMPREHENSION   C. Drawing Conclusions

DIRECTIONS: Read each selection. Then, answer the question following it after drawing a conclusion from the text.

1. Mother sent six-year-old Raymond on an errand to the post office. Full of importance, he ran, cutting across the back yard into that of a neighbor to reach his destination. His oldest sister called out to him, "Raymond, wait for me!" Although he was younger, she liked to follow her brother. Raymond had other ideas. "I can't hear you," he shouted back as he kept running.

    Why did Raymond say he could not hear his big sister?

    _____

2. They had missed the bus. The next one would not be along for another hour. The teenage girl knew she could walk the mile and a half home in less time than that. She took the hand of her five-year-old sister, for whom she described the walk ahead as an exciting adventure. Halfway home, the young one stopped, yanked off her hat, and said, "My feet hurt!"

    a. What had the teenage girl overlooked?

    _____

    b. Why did the little one yank off her hat?

    _____

3. Robbie arrived home from college for the holiday. Although no one was there to greet him, the odors from the kitchen did. He peeked into the oven where a fat, browning turkey greeted his eyes and nose. So did the pumpkin pies on the shelf and a big bowl of his mother's special cranberry sauce.

    What was the occasion of Robbie's homecoming?

    _____

COMPREHENSION   **D. Reading for Verification**

DIRECTIONS: Read the following classified advertisements. Answer the questions after verifying the information in the ads.

A. BUTCHERS (2) Full time & part time. Good sal. Apply in person: Ottomani Bros. Meat Market, 303 Rte 84, Sanford	**E.** LOST AND FOUND Lost Abyssinian cat. 1 yr. old. Vic So. Bwy, Kyack. Please call 835-7788
B. FOOD SERVICE positions for school cafeteria in Landrock County. Reg. & substitutes. For app't call 593-5054	**F.** Found white cat—white flea collar. Call 419-9395
C. RECEPTIONIST—CLERK TYPIST Southvale, good salary, benefits. Full time. Call 102-676-0043 X3	**G.** Lost cat: female, calico-orange, white and black, green collar, vic of Kyack. Call 149-853-1111
D. GAS STATION ATTENDANTS. Must be exp'd, over 18 years old. Apply in person. Seymon Shell, 3 Remsen Ave., Wildwood.	**H.** GAS ATTENDANT No exp necessary. All shifts avail. Apply: Gears Auto Center, Arctic, N.Y.

1. Your cousin tells you he saw a want ad for a butcher and that you could apply for the job by telephone. You don't quite believe him, so you check the newspaper ads.

   a. Was he right? Explain.

   _____

   b. What other misinformation did he give you?

   _____

2. Joan wants to work regularly in a school cafeteria. Should she answer the ad? Why?

   _____

3. You found a cat with a green collar. Your mother tells you that several lost cats are listed in the daily paper. Which one of the above ads will you answer?

   _____

4. You've never had a job but you would like to work now. You like cars and everything about them. Which of the two ads would you answer? Why?

   _____

5. Where is the job for receptionist-clerk typist?

   _____

COMPREHENSION   D. Reading for Verification

DIRECTIONS: Read the following classified advertisements. Answer the questions after verifying the information in the ads.

A. Security Officers **WELLS FARGO** The nation's largest security co. is recruiting for full-time positions in the Nreffus, P.I. area. High starting rate. Co. paid benefits. Only career minded indiv. need apply. For appt contact 222-2472	**C.** SALES: A chain of retail wall-paper stores looking for bright self-starting people. Full and part time. Call Mrs. Black 535-8020
	D. SHOE SALES PERSON Must be able to work mornings and weekends. Call 326-8838
B. WAREHOUSE WORKER, full-time daily 8AM-5PM. Some lifting of ceramic tile, writing orders, taking cash. Mr. Belg 253-6672	**E.** SHIPPING Immed opening. Some exp pref'd. Good sal & benefits. Toy manufacturer, Seyram, N.J. 200-723-0062

1. You're looking for a part-time job while you study architecture. Should you apply for the job in ad A? Why?

    _____

2. Which ad wants a person who is able to work mornings? Selling what?

    _____

3. Is the job for selling wallpaper with a small or large outfit? How can you tell?

    _____

4. For which ad should a person with a back problem not apply? Why?

    _____

5. You would like to work for a toy manufacturer. Which ad would you look into? What department would you have to be willing to work in?

    _____

COMPREHENSION   D. Reading for Verification

DIRECTIONS: Read the following classified advertisements. After verifying the information given in the ads, indicate whether the statements below are True or False.

APPLIANCES—SERVICES—SALES	BLACKTOP PAVING—SEALING
B&W Repair—Installation Washer-Dryer; Dishwash; Air Cond.; Stove. All makes, 1 yr guar. Call 7 days. $12 SERVICE CHARGE 453-3602	GALES PAVING Driveways—Topsoil & Gravel. FREE ESTIMATES 452-9160
DITCH DIGGING—EXCAVATING	CARPENTRY
EXCAVATING & SEWERS, Drainage, Dry Wells & Water Lines. Licensed. Bill Romaine: 537-0227; 753-2692 eve.	ALL TYPES OF WORK. Carpentry, Electrical, Plumbing, Painting. HO6-1910, No Job Too Small. 429-4779
FUEL OIL	MASONRY
LANDROCK FUEL OIL CO., INC. HOME & INDUSTRIAL FUEL Complete heating service, 54 years. Business & Homes—EP 5-1104 & 453-6784	All kinds of fireplaces. Brick & stone & concrete work. All types of repair. Call Tony 653-5044
	MOVING—TRUCKING—STORAGE
PAINTING	FLAGG BROS. Low Cost. Moving & Storage. Large or small. Anytime or anywhere. 866-1629 or 121-6550
H & L PAINTING: fully insured, free estimates. LOWEST PRICES! Call: 753-3205, 753-1267	

_____   1. If you call B & W Repair-Installation to check your air conditioner, even if there is nothing wrong with it, you will have to pay $12.

_____   2. Gales Paving will charge you to estimate how much a paving job will cost.

_____   3. You should call 429-4779 if you have a very small electrical job to be done.

_____   4. Bill Romaine can be reached during the day only.

_____   5. Landrock Fuel Oil Co. is a brand-new business.

_____   6. You can call Tony to come to repair your chimney.

_____   7. Flagg Bros. will move anything, anytime, anywhere.

_____   8. H & L Painting claim their prices are lowest.

_____   9. Do not call the Flagg Bros. if you want to put something in storage.

_____   10. Landrock Fuel services businesses as well as homes.

COMPREHENSION   D. Reading for Verification

DIRECTIONS: The following specifications are taken from patterns for various garments. From the information given, indicate whether the statements that pertain to them are True or False.

A.   PATTERN 10B6
        FABRICS—Cotton types: Broadcloth, chambray, seersucker, chino, poplin. Extra fabric needed to match plaids, stripes, one-way designs. Do not use obvious diagonal fabrics.

_____   1. You will need the same amount of fabric whether you make this garment of plain poplin or of striped poplin.

_____   2. A stretch fabric is recommended.

_____   3. A diagonal fabric should be used.

B.   PATTERN 200A
        FABRICS: Soft or crisp fabrics such as kettlecloth, linen, muslin, chambray, and lightweight denim. Obvious diagonal fabrics are not suitable. Allowance for matching plaids and stripes not included in yardages given.

_____   4. A heavy denim could be used.

_____   5. Additional yardage will have to be bought if the garment is made in striped material.

C.   PATTERN 3840
        Pullover blouses have extended shoulder lines. Blouse X with front opening has standing collar extending into ties. Blouse Y has a softly draped front. Blouse Z has a squared neckline and short, turned-up kimono sleeves. Purchased belt is optional.

_____   6. A belt pattern is included.

_____   7. For a blouse that ties with a bow, choose Blouse X.

_____   8. Blouse Z has a softly draped front and draped sleeves.

_____   9. Blouse Y has short, turned-up sleeves.

_____   10. All blouses have a buttoned opening.

COMPREHENSION   **E. Locating Information**   **1. *Reference material***
                                                 a. Can read and interpret
                                                 graphs

DIRECTIONS: The Acme Company graphed the number of units it sold during the week of April 8-12. Examine the graph carefully. Read the questions and write your answers on the blank lines.

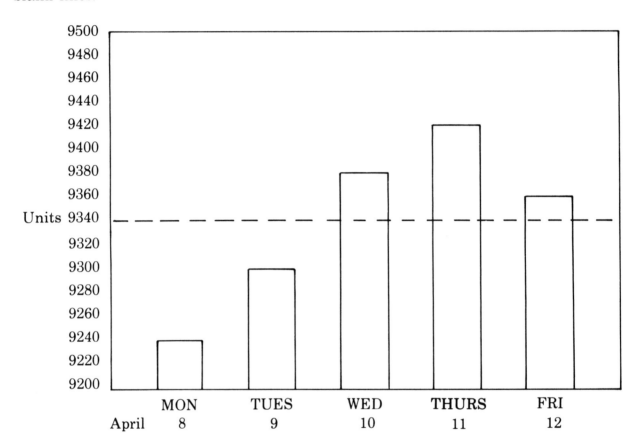

1.   How many units were sold on Monday?_____
2.   On what day was the greatest number of units sold? _____
3.   How many were sold on that day?_____
4.   Which day showed the greatest increase of the week?_____
5.   Were there any two days that had identical increases?_____
6.   Did the week end lower or higher than it started? _____
7.   What does the broken line at 9340 units represent? _____
8.   By how many units did Tuesday increase over Monday?_____
9.   What is the difference in units between Thursday and Friday? _____
10. On how many days was the number of units sold above the average? _____

Name: _____ Date: _____

COMPREHENSION   **E. Locating Information**   **1.** *Reference material*
                                                a. Can read and interpret
                                                    graphs

DIRECTIONS: Mr. Smith made a graph of the grade level reading achievement of his sixth grade classes. Examine the graph with care and then answer the questions pertaining to it. Write your answers on the blanks provided.

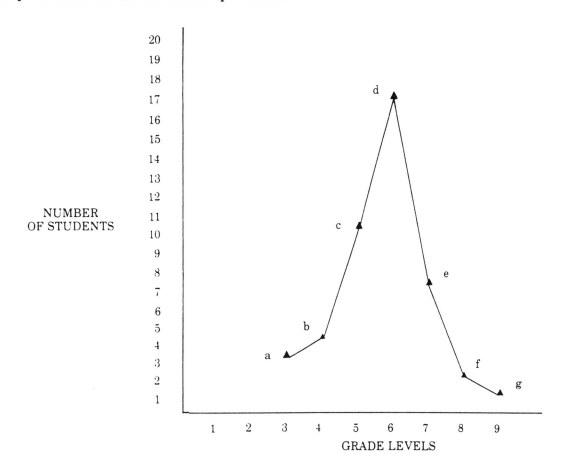

1. How many students are reading at their grade level? _____
2. How many students are reading below their grade level? _____
3. Are there any students above their grade level? How many? _____
4. What is the lowest level of any of the students? _____
5. What is the highest level achieved? _____
6. How many students have reached the eighth level? _____
7. What is the total number of students in grade 6? _____
8. Is the greatest span in the numbers of students between b and c or c and d?

_____

9. Is the shortest span between a and b or f and g? _____
10. The students at what points need the most help? _____

COMPREHENSION   **E. Locating Information**   **1.** *Reference material*
a. Can read and interpret
graphs

DIRECTIONS: The accompanying graph shows the number of companies whose stocks (issues) were either sold or bought (active) during the week. Study the graph and then answer the questions on the blanks.

1. How many issues were active on Monday? _____

2. What was the greatest number of issues active during the week? (Give the range.)

---

3. How would you describe the increase between Wednesday and Thursday? _____

4. The decrease between which days involved three issues? _____

5. What does the broken line at 832 represent? _____

6. How many days were above average? _____

7. How many days were below average? _____

8. Which day does the graph indicate was the most active? _____

9. Which day does the graph indicate was the least active? _____

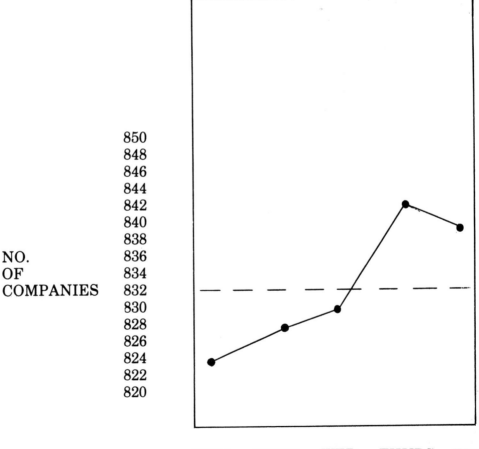

NO.
OF
COMPANIES

850
848
846
844
842
840
838
836
834
832
830
828
826
824
822
820

MON   TUES   WED   THURS   FRI

COMPREHENSION   **E. Locating Information**   **1. *Reference material***
a. Can read and interpret graphs

DIRECTIONS: The graph below represents attendance at the movie theater, the Gem, during the week of March 15-21. Study the graph and then answer the questions, putting your answers in the blanks provided.

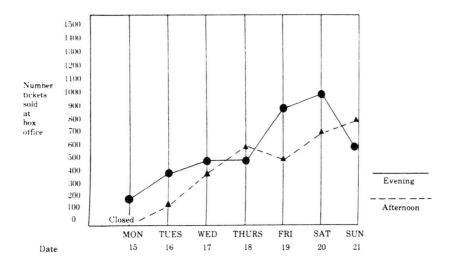

1. On what day of the week did the Gem Theater have the best evening attendance?

   _____

2. Which evening had the lowest attendance?

   _____

3. Does evening attendance remain the same or does it level off at any time?

   _____

4. Between which two evenings is the biggest increase in attendance?

   _____

5. Between which evenings is the sharpest decrease?

   _____

6. Does the theater ever reach capacity?

   _____

7. On which day was the afternoon attendance 100 people higher than the evening attendance?

   _____

8. Did afternoon attendance ever exceed evening attendance by more than 100 people?

   _____

9. Would it be accurate to say that afternoon attendance parallels evening attendance?

   _____

10. The greatest difference between afternoon and evening attendance occurs on:

   _____

COMPREHENSION   E. Locating Information   1. *Reference material*
                                           b. Can read and interpret
                                           maps

DIRECTIONS: Examine the map on the next page carefully. Note the general aspects and the details. Then, answer the following questions.

1. How would you get from Jamestown to Newport?

   _____

2. Is the well-known Ocean Avenue in the northernmost section or the southernmost

   section of Newport?

   _____

3. What street becomes what route that leads to Providence?

   _____

4. From Old Stone Mill, how would you get to "The Breakers"?

   _____

5. City Hall is between two famous landmarks. Which one is in the zone south of City

   Hall?

   _____

6. At the junction of which two roads is the National Tennis Hall of Fame?

   _____

7. What United States military installation is found on Coasters Harbor Island?

   _____

8. Name the island nearest to "downtown" Newport.

   _____

9. To what city does East Main Road or Route 138 lead going east?

   _____

10. What bay is on the west shore of Newport?

   _____

DIRECTIONS: This map is to be used with the exercise on page 131.

SOURCE: Adapted from the Rhode Island Official Highway Map. Prepared and issued by Rhode Island Development Council.

COMPREHENSION   **E. Locating Information**   **1.** *Reference material*
b. Can read and interpret
maps

DIRECTIONS: Manhattan, the heart of New York City, is an island. The map shown on the next page is of the southern tip of the island. Examine the map closely and then answer the questions that follow.

1. At the tip of Manhattan is _____ Park.

2. Another famous part of New York City, Brooklyn, is connected to Manhattan by

   a _____ and by a _____ .

3. Match the abbreviations with what they stand for:

   LA. _____   ST. _____   R.R. _____   CEM. _____
   AL. _____   U.S. _____   PL. _____   PK. _____

   a. Cemetery   b. Lane   c. Park   d. Street
   e. Place   f. Railroad   g. United States   h. Alley

4. The only street which originates at the tip of Battery Park and goes straight

   north is _____ .

5. A street with which the whole world represents American business and finance

   starts at Broadway between Pine and _____ and extends to South

   Street. It is the famous _____ Street.

6. Would the Manhattan Railroad coming from the west into the city be on a bridge

   or in a tunnel? _____ .

7. On both the east and the west side, a street is indicated as being _____ .

8. The space delineated by BULKHEAD and PIERHEAD is property belonging to

   the _____ .

9. The many piers that line both sides of the island suggest that there is much

   _____ activity in this part of the city.

10. The office of the mayor of the city would be expected to be found in a building

    near _____ Park.

DIRECTIONS: This map is to be used with the exercise on page 133.

SOURCE: Adapted from a map prepared and published by the City Planning Commission, Department of City Planning, New York City. Used with permission.

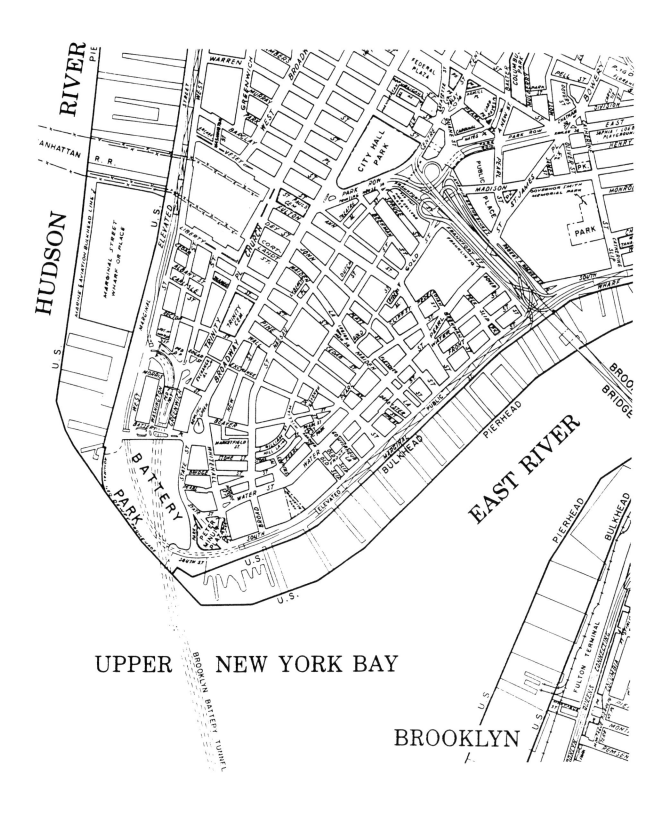

COMPREHENSION   E. Locating Information   1. *Reference material*
b. Can read and interpret maps

DIRECTIONS: Study the map and the map symbols on the next page very carefully. Then, answer the questions.

1. _____ and _____ Counties have their boundary in the middle of the _____ River.

2. _____ is an incorporated village on the west bank of the Hudson which includes part of the river.

3. The main U.S. route in this area is _____ .

4. Running diagonally across the southwest corner of the map is a _____ boundary.

5. The county road to that state (New Jersey) is route _____. It begins at U.S. route _____ . In New York, the route is called _____ .

6. Name one incorporated village located on the east bank of the Hudson River in Westchester County: _____ .

7. Name the state park found in Westchester County: _____ .

8. _____ Camp is located southwest of Tallman Mountain State Park.

9. There is a divided highway with a wide mall that crosses the state line and is called the Palisades _____ .

10. _____ State Park covers a large part of this area. Nearest the river, it appears to be _____ .

DIRECTIONS: This map is to be used with the exercise on page 135.

SOURCE: Adapted from a map prepared and published by the New York State Department of Transportation, in cooperation with the U.S. Department of Transportation, Federal Highway Administration.

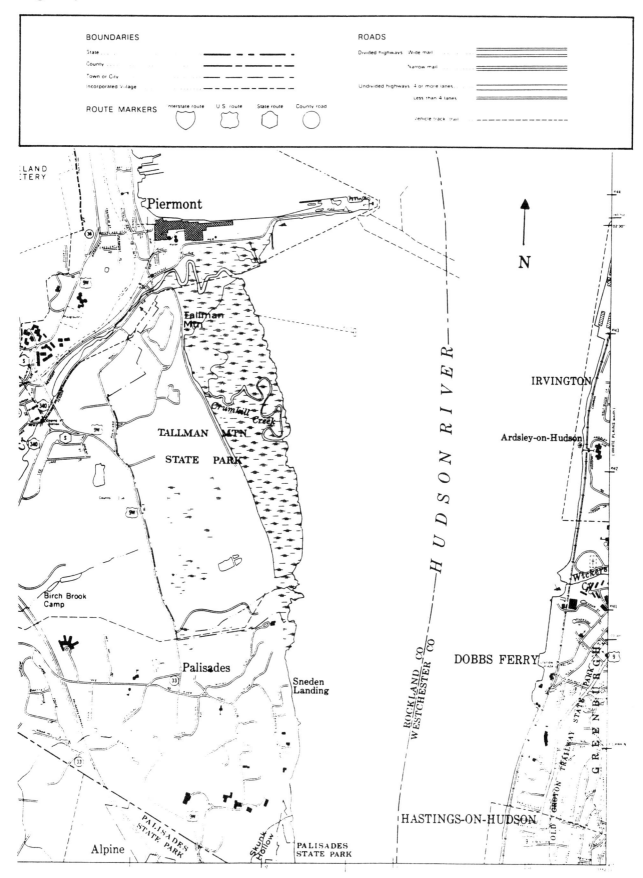

COMPREHENSION   **E. Locating Information**   1. *Reference material*
                                               b. Can read and interpret
                                               maps

DIRECTIONS: Examine the map on the next page, including the map symbols, very carefully. Then, answer the questions below by filling in the blanks.

1. On this map, the state boundary is also the boundary between two _____,

   the United States and _____.

2. There is a city of Niagara Falls in the Province of _____ ,

   Canada, as well as in the State of _____ , U.S.A.

3. Part of the boundary between Canada and the United States at this point is in the

   middle of the _____ .

4. Identify three falls at the bend of the river: _____ ,

   _____ , and _____ .

5. Give six different names of islands located in the area of the falls.

   1. _____   2. _____   3. _____

   4. _____   5. _____   6. _____

6. Based on the map, _____ Falls seems to be the largest falls, and

   lies mostly in _____ .

7. Does a railroad link the two cities of Niagara Falls? _____ If so,

   where is it in relation to the Falls? _____ .

8. On what city street is the YMCA located? _____

9. What major roadway skirts the entire riverfront of Niagara Falls, U.S.A.?

   _____

10. At both international crossings, what governmental offices are to be found?

    _____

SOURCE: Adapted from a map prepared and published by the New York State Department of Transportation, in cooperation with the U.S. Department of Transportation, Federal Highway Administration.

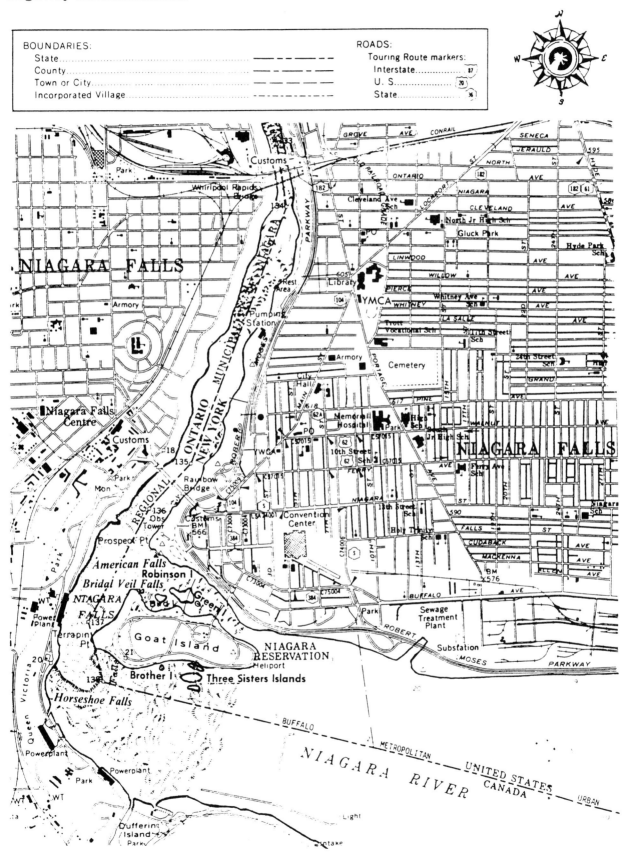

COMPREHENSION   E. Locating Information   **1.** *Reference material*
c. Can locate materials in
encyclopedia

DIRECTIONS: Write the volume number of the encyclopedia and the key word or words you would use to locate information on each of the following topics.

A And	Ane Az	B Bly	Bna Byz	C Cik	Cil Czu	D	E	F	G Gar	Gas Gy	Ha Hon	Hov I	J	K	La Luc	Lud Lyt	Ma Mil	Mim Mz	N	O	P Pil	Pim Py	Q	R	Sa Si	Sk Sz	T	U V W	X Y Z
1	2	3	4	5	6	7	8	9	10	11	12	13	14	15	16	17	18	19	20	21	22	23	24	25	26	27	28	29	30

1. Henry W. Longfellow's most famous work   _____   _____

2. Location of the Baseball Hall of Fame   _____   _____

3. Nickname of Texas   _____   _____

4. Galaxies   _____   _____

5. History of Cologne Cathedral   _____   _____

6. Evolution of rock music   _____   _____

7. Author of *The Hunchback of Notre Dame*   _____   _____

8. Biographical information for Christopher Fry   _____   _____

9. Year of the first telecast   _____   _____

10. Year of the first motion picture   _____   _____

COMPREHENSION   **E. Locating Information**   **1. *Reference material***
    c. Can locate materials in encyclopedia

DIRECTIONS: Write the volume number of the encyclopedia and the key word or words you would use to locate information on each of the following topics.

A / And	Ane / Az	B / Blv	Bna / Bvz	C / Cik	Cii / Czu	D	E	F	G / Gar	Gas / Gv	Ha / Hon	Hov / I	J	K	La / Luc	Lud / Lyt	Ma / Mil	Mim / Mz	N	O	P / Pil	Pim / Py	Q	R	Sa / Si	Sk / Sz	T	U V W	X Y Z
1	2	3	4	5	6	7	8	9	10	11	12	13	14	15	16	17	18	19	20	21	22	23	24	25	26	27	28	29	30

1. Year of the first moon landing   _____   _____

2. Drilling for oil   _____   _____

3. Major credit cards   _____   _____

4. Buddhism   _____   _____

5. Erich Fromm's field of work   _____   _____

6. Dates of birth and death of Albert Schweitzer   _____   _____

7. Famous operettas   _____   _____

8. Zen   _____   _____

9. Artists who practiced pointillism   _____   _____

10. Inventor of the daguerreotype   _____   _____

COMPREHENSION   **E. Locating Information**   1. *Reference material*
c. Can locate materials in
   encyclopedia

DIRECTIONS: Write the volume number of the encyclopedia and the key word or words you would use to locate information on each of the following topics.

A / And	Ane / Az	B / Bly	Bna / Byz	C / Cik	Cil / Czu	D	E	F	G / Gar	Gas / Gy	Ha / Hon	Hov / I	J	K	La / Luc	Lud / Lyt	Ma / Mil	Mim / Mz	N	O	P / Pil	Pim / Py	Q	R	Sa / Si	Sk / Sz	T	U V W	X Y Z
1	2	3	4	5	6	7	8	9	10	11	12	13	14	15	16	17	18	19	20	21	22	23	24	25	26	27	28	29	30

1.   Inventor of the steam engine   _____   _____

2.   Why Williamsburg is famous   _____   _____

3.   The major export of Argentina   _____   _____

4.   Songs written by Irving Berlin   _____   _____

5.   The witches of Old Salem   _____   _____

6.   Who Oedipus was   _____   _____

7.   What oceanography is   _____   _____

8.   Battles fought in ancient Thebes   _____   _____

9.   Gunsmithing   _____   _____

10.   The works of Ellery Queen   _____   _____

COMPREHENSION   E. Locating Information   1. *Reference material*
c. Can locate materials in encyclopedia

DIRECTIONS: Write the volume number of the encyclopedia and the key word or words you would use to locate information on each of the following topics.

A And	Ane Az	B Bly	Bna Bvz	C Cik	Cil Czu	D	E	F	G Gar	Gas Gv	Ha Hon	Hov I	J	K	La Luc	Lud Lyt	Ma Mil	Mim Mz	N	O	P Pil	Pim Py	Q	R	Sa Si	Sk Sz	T	U V W	X Y Z
1	2	3	4	5	6	7	8	9	10	11	12	13	14	15	16	17	18	19	20	21	22	23	24	25	26	27	28	29	30

1. The Tony Awards   _____   _____

2. The works of Omar Khayyam   _____   _____

3. What constitutes an antique   _____   _____

4. When the Beatles became famous   _____   _____

5. The achievements of Mark Antony   _____   _____

6. Styles of furniture   _____   _____

7. What hagiography is   _____   _____

8. The most famous work of Joyce Kilmer   _____   _____

9. The provinces of Mexico   _____   _____

10. How the Pyramids of Egypt were built   _____   _____

COMPREHENSION   **E. Locating Information**   **1. *Reference material***
d. Uses dictionary regularly

DIRECTIONS: Use your dictionary to check the correct syllabication of the following. Write the word divided into syllables in the space provided.

1.   silhouetted   _____
2.   arduous   _____
3.   primitive   _____
4.   enact   _____
5.   authenticity   _____

DIRECTIONS: In a dictionary, find the meaning of each word, write the definition, and then use the word in a sentence.

6. avid _____

_____

7. amplify _____

_____

8. massive _____

_____

9. staid _____

_____

10. retrieve _____

_____

COMPREHENSION   E. Locating Information   1. *Reference material*
                                                 d. Uses dictionary regularly

DIRECTIONS: Using a dictionary, find a synonym for each of the following words.

1.   barter   _____

2.   fascinate   _____

3.   philanthropy   _____

4.   fad   _____

5.   grovel   _____

DIRECTIONS: Using a dictionary, find and write the phonetic spelling and the meaning of each of the following words.

6.   rendezvous   _____   _____

7.   replica   _____   _____

8.   coyote   _____   _____

9.   decathlon   _____   _____

10. finale   - _____   _____

11. decade   _____   _____

12. labyrinth   _____   _____

13. grimace (verb) _____   _____

14. docile   _____   _____

15. rococo   _____   _____

COMPREHENSION **E. Locating Information** **1. *Reference material***
d. Uses dictionary regularly

DIRECTIONS: Using a dictionary, find and write the phonetic spelling and the meaning of each of the following words.

1. intimate (verb) _____ _____

2. succinct _____ _____

3. perjure _____ _____

4. acrid _____ _____

5. excruciating _____ _____

DIRECTIONS: In a dictionary, (1) find the meaning of the word, (2) find a synonym, and (3) write a sentence using the word or its synonym.

6. guardian _____

_____

7. skirmish (noun) _____

_____

8. rivalry _____

_____

9. banter (noun) _____

_____

10. amateur _____

COMPREHENSION   **E. Locating Information**   **2. *Library skills***
                                                 a. Uses card catalog

DIRECTIONS: Examine the three cards. Then, circle the correct answers below.

A

```
F  The whistling cow
B
   Bishop, Ray
        The whistling cow's problems
   Union Press 1980. illus.
   125 p.
        In this story, illustrated with
   cartoons, Betsy, the whistling cow,
   does strange things besides give
   milk.
   1. Cows-Stories  2. Animals Fiction I Title
```

B

```
B    LEE, ROBERT E.
L  Gray, Robert
        Robert E. Lee and his difficult
   decision, illus. by Andrew Mruk.
   Pioneer Press 1979.
        205 p. illus. (Great Men books)

        The biography of the man whose
   difficult decision led to leadership.
   1, Lee, Robert E.      I Title
```

C

```
796        BASKETBALL
G
   Girvin, Sarah, M.A.
        Girls' basketball; including
   summary of official rules.
   Forest Books 1978

   146 p.

   1. Basketball          I Title
```

1. If you wanted to know how many Shakespeare plays were in the library, under which category would you search?

   a. Plays   b. Romeo and Juliet   c. Shakespeare   d. English literature

2. Which of the three cards indicates that its subject is fiction?

   a. Card A   b. Card B   c. Card C   d. None

3. The top line of a catalog card printed in all capital letters indicates:

   a. author   b. title   c. shelf   d. subject

4. The call number of Card C is:

   a. Basketball   b. 796 G   c. Girls   d. Girvin

5. Which of the three cards indicates that its book is a biography?

   a. None   b. Card A   c. Card B   d. Card C

6. Which card describes a book that is illustrated with cartoons?

   a. Card A   b. Card B   c. Card C   d. None

7. Which card describes a book that is part of a series?

   a. Card A   b. Card B   c. Card C   d. None

8. Except on the author card, on which line does the author's name appear?

   a. First   b. Second   c. Third   d. Last

9. Under which two other listings would you look for the book on Basketball?

   a. Author—Girvin   b. Title   c. Rules

10. Which card indicates that its book has the greatest number of pages?

    a. None   b. Card C   c. Card B   d. Card A

COMPREHENSION   **E. Locating Information**   **2.** *Library skills*
a. Uses card catalog

DIRECTIONS: Examine the three cards and then answer the questions on the blanks.

A
```
531 The lever and the pulley
A
      Albert, Luke
           The lever and the pulley make man's
    work easier. Illustrated by the author.
    New York, Pit Press c. 1976
    146 p. illus.

           The book shows how a lever works;
    it also demonstrates the pulley's function.
    Several practical applications are
    explained and illustrated.

    1. Physics applied        I Title
```

B
```
796           AUTOMOBILE RACING
C
      Condon, Denis
           A high on speed. Photographs by
    Art Theme.
    New York, Pit Books c. 1963
       200 p. illus.

           "The author writes about the thrill
    he gets when driving at high speed in com-
    petitions, including his feelings before
    and after the race."

       1.   Automobile racing      I Title
```

C
```
821 Pumper, Gus
P
               Sorry we're out of gas.
    Short stories. Herhigh 1975
    185 p.

           A college freshman relating his
    humorous experiences working in a
    gasoline station during the gasoline
    shortage shows human nature under
    crisis.
    I.    Title
```

1. Write the call number of the author card. _____

2. Card B is the _____ card.

3. Which author illustrated his own book? _____

4. Which card is a title card? _____

5. Is there a card for a book of fiction among these cards? _____

6. Which book title has a different publisher? Name it. _____

7. Give the title of the book that is about physics. _____

8. Which card indicates that its book is not subjective, that it does not reflect the author's own feelings, opinions, or experiences? _____

9. What do the letters under the numbers in the margins of all these cards indicate? _____

10. From these books, if you were looking for a book to make you laugh and relax, which call letters would you use? _____

   Which would you use for more exciting reading? _____

Name: _____ Date: _____

DIRECTIONS: The sketch represents a card catalog. Use it to find answers to the questions below. Indicate, by circling your answer, in which drawer you would look to find the following information.

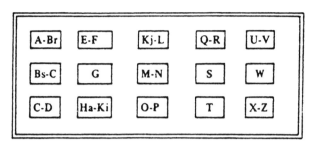

1. Books written by Phil Brennan

        O-P   Bs-C   A-Br   E-F

2. A history about Las Vegas

        U-V   Kj-L   G   Ha-Ki

3. The title card for *The Piano Tuner*

        M-N   W   T   O-P

4. A book about mythology

        A-Br   Bs-C   M-N   U-V

5. The books written by Sinclair Lewis

        S   Kj-L   Bs-C   W

6. The author of *How Green Was My Valley*

        G   U-V   M-N   Ha-Ki

7. Number of pages in the book *The Bridge Over the River Kwai*

        Kj-L   A-Br   Q-R   O-P

8. A book on vintage wines

        U-V   W   Bs-C   T

9. The history of lacrosse

        Ha-Ki   S   Bs-C   Kj-L

10. As much information as possible about the French author Victor Hugo

        E-F   A-Br   U-V   Ha-Ki

COMPREHENSION   E. Locating Information   2. *Library skills*
                                              a. Uses card catalog

DIRECTIONS: Write whether the statements below about card catalogs are True or False.

_____ 1. Subject cards have the top line printed in capital letters

_____ 2. The card with the author's name on top is the author card.

_____ 3. The letter *p* after a number indicates the number of pages in the book.

_____ 4. All cards briefly summarize what a book is about.

_____ 5. A card should indicate whether a book is illustrated.

_____ 6. The cards do not always specify whether the illustrations are cartoons, drawings, or photographs.

_____ 7. Fiction has no call number, merely the letter F.

_____ 8. Biography has a call number.

_____ 9. It is necessary to know all three—author, title, and subject—when looking up a book in the card catalog.

_____ 10. When neither title nor author are known, one must look up the subject.

COMPREHENSION   **E. Locating Information**   **2. *Library skills***
                                                  b. Understands book
                                                  classification system

DIRECTIONS: From the information in the following table, write the numbers for the library classifications of the following books.

000-099	Encyclopedias, Newspapers
100-199	Philosophy and Psychology
200-299	Religion-Mythology
300-399	Social Sciences—Government, Civil Liberties, Folklore, Legends
400-499	Languages
500-599	Science—Animals, Plants, Astronomy, Math
600-699	Applied Science—Farming, Space Travel, Flying, Homemaking
700-799	Fine Arts and Recreation—Music, Sports, Dramatics
800-899	Literature—Plays, Speeches, Essays, Poetry
900-999	History-Geography—Travel, Modern and Ancient History

_____   1.   *Cooking with a Microwave Oven*

_____   2.   *Bennett's Latin Grammar*

_____   3.   *How to Care for House Plants*

_____   4.   *Visit the Grand Canyon*

_____   5.   *Collected Works of Mark Twain*

_____   6.   *Modern Philosophies*

_____   7.   *Poems by Sara Teasdale*

_____   8.   *The History of Ancient Greece*

_____   9.   *The World Almanac*

_____   10.   *Space Explored*

COMPREHENSION   **E. Locating Information**   **2.** *Library skills*
b. Understands book
classification system

DIRECTIONS: Using the table, write the numbers for the library classifications of the following books.

000-099	Encyclopedias, Newspapers
100-199	Philosophy and Psychology
200-299	Religion-Mythology
300-399	Social Sciences—Government, Civil Liberties, Folklore, Legends
400-499	Languages
500-599	Science—Animals, Plants, Astronomy, Math
600-699	Applied Science—Farming, Space Travel, Flying, Homemaking
700-799	Fine Arts and Recreation—Music, Sports, Dramatics
800-899	Literature—Plays, Speeches, Essays, Poetry
900-999	History-Geography—Travel, Modern and Ancient History

_____   1. *The Waist Watcher Cooks*

_____   2. *How to Express Yourself Correctly*

_____   3. *Getting the Ball into the Basket*

_____   4. *Farming as a Career*

_____   5. *Decorating Your Home*

_____   6. *So You Want to Be a Coach?*

_____   7. *M Is for Music*

_____   8. *Learning Spanish Is Easy*

_____   9. *The Metric System Simplified*

_____   10. *Encyclopedia of Music*

Name: _____ Date: _____

COMPREHENSION   E. Locating Information   3. *Periodical reading*
                                                  a. Reads newspapers
                                                           regularly

DIRECTIONS: Read a newspaper article, either one assigned to you or one you have chosen. Then, answer the following questions about the article.

HEADLINE of the article:

_____

_____

_____

WHO?

_____

_____

WHERE?

_____

_____

WHEN?

_____

_____

WHAT?

_____

_____

HOW?

_____

_____

_____

COMPREHENSION   E. Locating Information   3. *Periodical reading*
                                              a. Reads newspapers
                                                 regularly

DIRECTIONS: Read an editorial in a current newspaper. Then, among the questions below, answer those which apply to what you have read.

Newspaper: _____

Title of editorial: _____

Date: _____

1. What news fact is the editorial about?

2. Is the writer for or against the issue? How can you tell?

3. What reasons are given for the position or point of view expressed?

4. Do you agree with the writer? Give your reasons.

Name: _____ Date: _____

COMPREHENSION   **E. Locating Information**   **3.** *Periodical reading*
                                                             b. Knows major sections of
                                                                 newspapers

DIRECTIONS: A Sunday newspaper usually has the following seven sections: A. the main one with the headline; B. local; C. business; D. sports; E. travel; M. magazine, T. TV magazine. The first page of section A provides the index, as shown here. Write the letter of the section of this newspaper in which you would find the answer to each question below.

INDEX

Action	1B
Ann Landers	Magazine
Around Rockland	Magazine
Business	Section C
Classified	Section C
Education	7B
For the Record	2D
Home Improvement	Magazine
News Roundup	4A
Obituaries	5B
Party Line	2B
People	1A
Rockland Business	1C
Senior Citizens	Magazine
Sports	Section D
Sports Viewpoint	4D
Television	TV/Radio Week
Travel	Section E
Viewpoint	14A
Week in Review	15A
What's Ahead	4B
Where to Go	Magazine
Young World	Magazine

1. News on national politics   _____

2. Ann Landers   _____

3. Latest developments in banking   _____

4. Saturday football game scores   _____

5. Off-season vacations   _____

6. Summary of the week's news (give page also)   _____

7. Topics of interest to teenagers   _____

8. The latest in the schools   _____

9. Ads for lost and found   _____

10. Local business news   _____

_____ 11. This index does not list Editorials. What word is used instead?

_____ 12. Where would you find movie times?

_____ 13. What appears under Obituaries?

_____ 14. Where would you find information about meetings and other happenings coming up during the week?

_____ 15. Would "Sports Viewpoint" be fact or opinion?

COMPREHENSION   E. Locating Information   3. *Periodical reading*
b. Knows major sections of newspapers

DIRECTIONS: With the help of TODAY'S INDEX below, answer the questions that follow.

TODAY'S INDEX

Annual Meeting Briefs	38	Foreign Markets	36, 46
Commodities	42	Gov't Agency Quotes	47
Corrections	4	Int'l News	34, 35
Credit Markets	41	Money Rates	41
Dividend News	39	NYSE Highs & Lows	51
Earnings Digest	21	Odd-Lot Trading	51
Editorials	30	Securities Markets	43-50
Financing Business	41	Tax-Exempts	41
Foreign Exchange	48	Who's News	38

_____ 1. On what page will you find the opinion of the editors on current issues?

_____ 2. You want to exchange American dollars for German marks and French francs. On what page should you look to find the rates?

_____ 3. There was a gross error printed in yesterday's paper. You, among others, brought it to the attention of the paper. Where should you look for the correction?

_____ 4. On what pages will international news be found?

_____ 5. On what page can one read about personalities of importance who have made the news?

_____ 6. In this newspaper, letters to the editor are printed on the page opposite the editorials. This page is referred to as the OP Ed page. What page would that be in this issue?

_____ 7. You want to know what happened at the annual meeting of the company your father works for. Where should you look?

_____ 8. An article is entitled, "Commodities: Easing of Credit at Rural Banks." On what page should it appear?

_____ 9. Where will you find an article about information given out by Moscow on its economy?

_____ 10. Major companies report what their operations have brought them in earnings over the period of a year. On which page will you find such information?

COMPREHENSION   **E. Locating Information**   **3. *Periodical reading***
                                                    c. Reads magazines regularly

DIRECTIONS: Over a period of time agreed to by you and your teacher, you will read several magazine articles on a topic of your own choice or one that is assigned to you. You will make a record of these readings on this sheet, which you will hand in to your teacher at the agreed-upon time.

Name of Magazine	Emphasis of Magazine	Title of Article Read	Author

On the reverse side of this sheet, in one sentence, either summarize what each article is about or describe something in the article that interested you very much.

COMPREHENSION   **E. Locating Information**   **3. *Periodical reading***
d. Uses periodicals for current
information

DIRECTIONS: Twelve magazine titles are listed here. Beneath them are ten topics. On the line next to each topic, write the letter for the magazine in which you would find an article on that topic.

A. *Antiques*

B. *Modern Photography*

C. *Opera News*

D. *Backpacker*

E. *American Baby*

F. *Journal of Negro History*

G. *Art Forum*

H. *Popular Electronics*

I. *National Geographic*

J. *Hobbies*

K. *Parents*

L. *Harvard Business Review*

_____ 1. The difficult job of parenting

_____ 2. Little-known outstanding achievements of black women

_____ 3. Collecting thimbles

_____ 4. Printed circuits and how they grew

_____ 5. The best places to look for antique guns

_____ 6. Will inflation end?

_____ 7. Leonard Bernstein's new opera

_____ 8. The latest development at Kodak

_____ 9. The Picasso exhibit in the U.S.

_____ 10. Favorite trails in local foothills

Name: _____ Date: _____

DIRECTIONS: Take this sheet to your school or local library. Make a list of magazines you find there and indicate the emphasis of each.

Magazine Title	Emphasis
1.	
2.	
3.	
4.	
5.	
6.	
7.	
8.	
9.	
10.	
11.	
12.	
13.	
14.	
15.	
16.	
17.	
18.	
19.	
20.	

Name: _____ Date: _____

COMPREHENSION   F. Can Read Proof Marks

DIRECTIONS: Read the following paragraph. Then, rewrite it with the corrections indicated by the proof marks.

Frozen Waterways

Since we are close to the bering Sea our inland waterways are affected by the tide. when the great freeze-up occurs, the waterways usually have a smooth ice cover. An exception occurs when the cold wind is strong and blows the freezing water into piles of "broken glass" along the windward shoreline. Once the surface is frozen hard and the tide begins to swell in under the ice, the swelling water underneath and the pressure from the weight of the snow above cause the ice to crack open and lift up into giant ledges in spots. The swelling water comes through the cracks and creates a new foamy ice cover along the river banks which freezes from the top and leaves open pockets underneath as the tide recedes. The kids love to walk on the ice pockets and crack them open. there is plenty of solid ice beneath so there is no danger.

_____
_____
_____
_____
_____
_____

(Use other side if necessary.)

COMPREHENSION   F. Can Read Proof Marks

DIRECTIONS: Read the following paragraph. Then, rewrite it with the corrections indicated by the proof marks.

The Family Room

Well planed, comfortable, and uncluttered - such should a family room be. furniture should be arranged and balanced for easy communication and dinning. a rug would add interest and create a focal point in front of the fireplace. The dinning area is away from family traffic. Yet keeps an easy corner of its own. The window wall has been kept uncurtained so that the veiw of the rolling hills is not lost.

_____
_____
_____
_____
_____
_____
_____
_____
_____
_____
_____
_____
_____

(Use other side if necessary.)

COMPREHENSION   **F. Can Read Proof Marks**

DIRECTIONS: Read the following paragraph. Then, rewrite it with the corrections indicated by the proof marks.

A Boy's Room

A boy's room in shades of sand and brown has a

whole wall of cork for basketball posters and photos.

desk and chest are mostly white with natural oak.

The only decorative elements are blinds in vanilla

striped with sand and brown for graphic interest,

taking from the sand and brown of the walls.

at night, they are closed for privacy. The comforter

repeats stripes and introduces blue

_____

_____

_____

_____

_____

_____

_____

_____

_____

_____

_____

_____

(Use other side if necessary.)

COMPREHENSION   **F. Can Read Proof Marks**

DIRECTIONS: Read the following paragraph. Then, rewrite it with the corrections indicated by the proof marks.

Optimistic

Optimistic enthusiasm is a ~~sickness~~ *malady* peculiar to

youth. In my short life, i have witnessed numerous

tragic events but I truely believe that our society

is stronger because of having to solve these problems.

Stronger because the problems are being faced, discussed,

and solutions are often found. I am optimistic about

the future because the immediate past, with all its problems,

has been favorable to me.

_____

_____

_____

_____

_____

_____

_____

_____

_____

_____

_____

_____

(Use other side if necessary.)

Answer Key

VOCABULARY
A. Word Recognition
1. Uses context clues
a. How the word is used in a sentence

Page 16
1. b	6. a
2. b	7. b
3. a	8. c
4. c	9. a
5. b	10. b

Page 17
1. c	6. a
2. b	7. a
3. a	8. b
4. c	9. a
5. b	10. b

Page 18
1. c	6. a
2. b	7. c
3. b	8. a
4. b	9. b
5. b	

Page 19
1. c	6. a
2. b	7. b
3. a	8. c
4. a	9. c
5. a	10. a

b. Function of the word

Page 20
1. b	5. b
2. b	6. c
3. c	7. a
4. a	8. c

Page 21
1. b	6. b
2. b	7. c
3. a	8. c
4. c	9. c
5. c	

Page 22
1. b	6. b
2. c	7. a
3. b	8. a
4. b	9. b
5. a	

Page 23
1. a	6. c
2. b	7. b
3. a	8. a
4. c	9. c
5. c	10. b

2. Uses configuration clues
a. Visual impressions of words

Page 24
1. j	6. a
2. h	7. i
3. f	8. d
4. c	9. b
5. e	10. g

Page 25
1. g	6. h
2. e	7. b
3. a	8. f
4. i	9. c
5. j	10. d

Page 26
1. g	6. i
2. d	7. j
3. a	8. e
4. f	9. c
5. b	10. h

Page 27
1. f	6. d
2. e	7. h
3. b	8. j
4. i	9. a
5. c	10. g

269

Answer Key

b. Shape, length of words

Page 28
1. f
2. b
3. j
4. e
5. c
6. d
7. i
8. g
9. a
10. h
11. o
12. p
13. n
14. q
15. t
16. s
17. m
18. k
19. l
20. r

Page 29
1. excited
2. Declaration
3. discharge
4. fists
5. faded
6. Halt
7. curable
8. dislocated
9. dummy
10. entertain
11. express
12. appreciate

Page 30
1. apply
2. calcium
3. commonly
4. Communism
5. polite
6. contract
7. roller
8. disposition
9. emperor
10. formation
11. extremely
12. gems

Page 31
1. generations
2. head-on
3. individual
4. newspaperman
5. Moslem
6. lowlands
7. meter
8. offshore
9. patents
10. drugstore
11. pound
12. expensive

3. Uses language rhythms
a. Rhyming clues

Page 32
1. all
2. earth, birth
3. all
4. tear, fear, here
5. none
6. all
7. loan, stone, bone
8. fey, gray, they
9. cry, sigh, die
10. none

Page 33
1. nutty, putty, rutty
2. none
3. post, toast, host
4. oar, soar, more
5. all
6. hockey, jockey, perky
7. all
8. all
9. none
10. hoot, shoot, root
11. all
12. coil, foil, boil

Page 34
1. vanity-sanity
2. boast-toast
3. old-cold
4. puzzle-nuzzle
5. flutter-shutter
6. middle-fiddle
7. charity-parity
8. prudent-student
9. cast-fast
10. eight-ate
11. jazz-razz
12. hockey-jockey

Page 35
1. dreary-cheery
2. setting-forgetting
3. beauty-duty
4. stifling-rifling
5. merrily-verily
6. baking-raking
7. ox-fox
8. moan-lone
9. comb-dome
10. broad-applaud
11. zoned-toned
12. soccer-locker

b. Appreciation for general rhythm of well-expressed ideas

Page 36
1. B
2. A
3. B
4. B
5. A
6. B
7. A
8. B
9. B
10. B
11. A
12. A

Page 37
1. c
2. e
3. a
4. f
5. b
6. d
7. l
8. g
9. h
10. i
11. j
12. k

Page 38
1. X
2. X
3. X
4. O
5. O
6. X
7. X
8. X
9. O
10. X

Page 39
1. O
2. O
3. X
4. X
5. O
6. X
7. X
8. X
9. O
10. O

B. Knows and Uses Prefixes and Suffixes

Page 40		
1. speak	16. state	
2. week	17. emotion	
3. hero	18. wealth	
4. ministrat(e)	19. life	
5. class	20. spite	
6. cover	21. ment	
7. deduct	22. ness	
8. just	23. less	
9. magic	24. able	
10. patriot	25. ous	
11. coward	26. ward	
12. illusion	27. hood	
13. maid	28. ful	
14. politic	29. or	
15. predict	30. ic	

Page 41	
1. de	11. re
2. dis	12. dis
3. ad	13. circum
4. im	14. de
5. inter	15. inter
6. mis	16. mis
7. ir	17. re
8. non	18. pro
9. super	19. super
10. un	20. semi

Page 42	
1. able	11. ment, b
2. ence	12. ize, e
3. less	13. ward, g
4. ment	14. less, a
5. ize	15. ly, d
6. ment	16. ly, i
7. ly	17. izer, j
8. ward	18. or, h
9. ly	19. ly, f
10. y (en)	20. en, c

Page 43

	Prefix	Root Word	Suffix	Meaning
1.	bi	form		two
2.	de	frost		from
3.		trust	y	full of
4.		truth	ful	full of
5.	dis	approve		not
6.		metal	ic	made of
7.	circum	scribe		around
8.		liquid	fy	change to
9.		pure	ity	state of being
10.	de	grade		from
11.		bump	y	full of

	Prefix	Root Word	Suffix	Meaning
12.	mis	spell		wrong
13.		sane	ity	state of being
14.	inter	com		between
15.	ex	hale		out
16.		poet	ic	like or made of
17.		shake	en	one who is
18.	pre	dict		before
19.	post	script		after
20.		prime	ary	relating to

C. Word Meaning
1. Knows multiple meanings of words

Page 44		
1. b	6. a	
2. c	7. c	
3. a	8. b	
4. b	9. b	
5. a	10. c	

Page 45		
1. c	6. a	
2. b	7. c	
3. a	8. c	
4. a	9. a	
5. b	10. c	

Page 46		
1. a	6. c	
2. a	7. b	
3. a	8. a	
4. c	9. a	
5. c	10. c	

Page 47		
1. a	6. c	
2. c	7. a	
3. b	8. b	
4. a	9. a	
5. a	10. a	

2. Can associate words and feelings

Page 48		
1. awake	6. content	
2. amiable	7. burned	
3. affected	8. frivolous	
4. high	9. happy	
5. certain	10. submissive	

Page 49		
1. rude	6. cowardly	
2. sly	7. certain	
3. accompanied	8. depressed	
4. decisive	9. agreeable	
5. important	10. disturbed	

Answer Key

Page 50
1. d
2. f
3. b
4. a
5. e
6. h
7. o
8. m
9. n
10. l
11. p
12. k
13. s
14. t
15. u
16. x
17. w
18. v

Page 51
1. confident
2. kind
3. perplexed
4. offended
5. worn out
6. safe
7. terrified
8. tired
9. uncaring
10. downhearted
11. angry
12. sorry

3. Formal and informal language
a. Identifies speech patterns

Page 52
1. d
2. g
3. e
4. b
5. a
6. i
7. j
8. k
9. f
10. c

Page 53
1. identification
2. as if he owns the place (business)
3. contest
4. very angry
5. it was another matter
6. a lot of nonsense
7. asked his father to lend him fifty dollars
8. a lot of money
9. brawl
10. to be in charge

Page 54
1. formal
2. formal
3. colloquial
4. colloquial
5. formal
6. colloquial
7. colloquial
8. formal
9. colloquial
10. formal

Page 55
1. colloquial
2. formal
3. colloquial
4. formal
5. colloquial
6. colloquial
7. formal
8. colloquial
9. colloquial
10. formal

b. Understands level of language usage

Page 56
1. a
2. b
3. b
4. b
5. a
6. b
7. a
8. b
9. b
10. b

Page 57
1. b
2. a
3. b
4. a
5. a
6. a
7. b
8. a
9. a
10. a

Page 58
1. b
2. a
3. d
4. c
5. b
6. a
7. a
8. b

Page 59
1. c
2. c
3. d
4. a
5. b
6. d
7. c
8. b

4. Distinguishes between aided and unaided recall

Page 60
1. unaided
2. aided
3. unaided
4. unaided
5. unaided
6. aided
7. aided
8. aided
9. aided
10. aided

Page 61
1. aided
2. aided
3. unaided
4. aided
5. aided
6. unaided
7. aided
8. unaided
9. aided
10. aided

Page 62
1. unaided
2. aided
3. aided
4. aided
5. unaided
6. unaided
7. unaided
8. unaided
9. aided
10. unaided

Page 63
1. aided
2. aided
3. aided
4. aided
5. aided
6. aided
7. aided
8. aided
9. aided
10. unaided

5. Can hyphenate words

Page 64
1. meas-ure
2. up-turn
3. per-haps
4. ac-cent
5. moth-er
6. for-ward
7. sit-ting
8. chil-dren
9. po-lice
10. re-main

Page 65
1. set-tle
2. re-turn
3. quar-ter
4. thought-ful
5. ex-plode
6. com-ing
7. light-house
8. mil-lion
9. al-most
10. cer-tain

Page 66
1. can-non
2. sculp-ture
3. viv-id
4. ti-ny
5. star-fish
6. wet-ness
7. ma-rine
8. note-book
9. con-stant
10. dan-ger

Page 67
1. to-day
2. per-son
3. child-hood
4. he-ro
5. wom-an
6. won-der
7. fish-ing
8. par-ents
9. him-self
10. tea-spoon

6. Can provide synonyms

Page 68
1. question
2. none crossed out
3. shout
4. hide
5. life
6. gift
7. none crossed out
8. bird
9. none crossed out
10. none crossed out

Page 69
1. monster
2. gadget
3. reap
4. quick
5. madness
6. shy, timid
7. uncovered
8. praises, compliments
9. hole
10. feeling

Page 70
1. g
2. n
3. f
4. l
5. h
6. j
7. d
8. i
9. b
10. k

Page 71
1. change
2. decrease
3. important
4. scheme
5. continue
6. clever
7. forbid
8. stubborn
9. surroundings
10. amuse

7. Can provide antonyms

Page 72
1. poor
2. War
3. slow
4. slavery
5. rewards
6. mobile
7. dusk
8. minority
9. feet, foot, toe
10. desert

Page 73
1. f
2. l
3. a
4. i
5. k
6. c
7. j
8. d
9. e
10. g

Page 74
1. d
2. g
3. a
4. e
5. c
6. i
7. k
8. m
9. h
10. j

Page 75
1. military
2. ample
3. quiet
4. anger
5. short
6. bitter
7. give
8. redeem
9. reveal
10. ascent

8. Understands homophones

Page 76
1. seas, seize
2. one, won
3. scent, sent
4. weigh, way
5. shone, shown
6. yolk, yoke
7. hear, here
8. sight, site
9. heard, herd
10. him, hymn

Page 77 (Correct homophones)
1. bale
2. waste
3. beets
4. belle
5. deer
6. vein
7. you'll
8. fleas
9. foul
10. fir

Page 78
a. hair
b. hare
c. pale
d. pail
e. bare
f. bear
g. hire
h. higher
i. idle
j. idol
k. coarse
l. course
m. ring
n. wring
o. red
p. read
q. sale
r. sail
s. few
t. phew

Page 79
a. tee
b. tea
c. Pole
d. poll
e. dough
f. do
g. lode
h. load
i. peek
j. Peak
k. wear
l. Where
m. "Hi!"
n. high
o. chord
p. cord
q. altar
r. alter
s. dew
t. do

9. Understands homographs

Page 80
1. bore
2. close
3. pupils
4. bundle
5. permit
6. blue
7. bank
8. calf

Answer Key

Page 81
1. b
2. c
3. a
4. c
5. b
6. c
7. b
8. b
9. a
10. b

Page 82
1. hum
2. fancy
3. sink
4. dive
5. flag
6. hide
7. gun
8. furrow
9. perch
10. pet

Page 83
1. quarter
2. race
3. raw
4. pass
5. pan
6. pack
7. lick
8. letter
9. plate
10. iron

10. Can write metaphors
11. Can write similes

Page 84
1. metaphor
2. simile
3. metaphor
4. simile
5. metaphor
6. simile
7. metaphor
8. metaphor
9. metaphor
10. metaphor

Page 85
1. simile
2. metaphor
3. metaphor
4. metaphor
5. simile
6. simile
7. metaphor
8. metaphor
9. simile
10. simile

Page 86
and Page 87
For all exercises in writing metaphors, ascertain that there are comparisons and that these are implied. For all exercises in writing similes, ascertain that comparisons are expressed with *as* or *like*.

WORD ATTACK

A. *Phonic and Structural Characteristics of Words*

1. *Knows initial consonants and blends*

Page 88
1. s̲c, bl
2. b̲r, bl
3. s̲h, bl
4. blank
5. k̲, c
6. g̲, c
7. d̲r, bl
8. l̲, c
9. blank
10. f̲, c
11. s̲t, bl
12. c̲r, bl
13. blank
14. blank
15. w̲, c
16. z̲, c
17. t̲, c
18. t̲, c
19. s̲h, bl
20. blank

Page 89
1. f̲, c
2. blank
3. p̲l, bl
4. c̲, c
5. c̲l, bl
6. blank
7. c̲r, bl
8. d̲, c
9. f̲l, bl
10. n̲, c
11. blank
12. f̲l, bl
13. blank
14. w̲h, bl
15. z̲, c
16. t̲h, bl
17. w̲r, bl
18. f̲, c
19. s̲, c
20. t̲r, bl

Page 90
1. p̲, c
2. l̲, c
3. w̲r, bl
4. c̲, c
5. s̲h, bl
6. f̲, c
7. blank
8. m̲, c
9. p̲l, bl
10. t̲w, bl
11. j̲, c
12. blank
13. v̲, c
14. z̲, c
15. t̲r, bl
16. p̲r, bl
17. d̲r, bl
18. blank
19. t̲w, bl
20. r̲, c

Page 91
1. b̲r, bl
2. blank
3. g̲r, bl
4. t̲, c
5. n̲, c
6. blank
7. s̲l, bl
8. blank
9. p̲r, bl
10. g̲l, bl
11. blank
12. h̲, c
13. w̲r, bl
14. t̲, c
15. p̲l, bl
16. d̲w, bl
17. blank
18. t̲w, bl
19. s̲h, bl
20. r̲, c

2. *Knows short and long vowels*

Page 92
1. ā
2. ē
3. ō
4. ă
5. ĕ
6. ĭ
7. ŏ
8. ō
9. ŭ
10. ĭ

Page 93
1. ē
2. ĭ
3. ā
4. ĕ
5. ĭ
6. ŭ
7. ă
8. ō
9. ē
10. ŏ

Page 94
1. ĭ
2. ă
3. ŏ
4. ē
5. ŭ
6. ō
7. ĭ
8. ĕ
9. ā
10. ĭ

Page 95
1. ă
2. ō
3. ĭ
4. ē
5. ĭ
6. ī
7. ĕ
8. ā
9. ō
10. ŭ

B. *Vowel Sounds*
1. *Knows vowel rules*
a. *When there is only one vowel in a word or syllable, the vowel is short*

Page 96
1. ĕnd	6. hīgh
2. jŭst	7. whĕn
3. lōw	8. drŭnk
4. cŭrl	9. lănd
5. sĭx	10. shē

Page 97
1. tōe	6. āle
2. stămp	7. pŭck
3. hĭm	8. pŏwer
4. nŏvel	9. bŭst
5. ărid	10. dĕll

Page 98
1. A	6. A
2. B	7. A
3. A	8. B
4. B	9. A
5. B	10. B

Page 99
1. B	6. A
2. A	7. B
3. B	8. A
4. A	9. B
5. B	10. B

b. *When there are two vowels in a word or syllable, the first vowel is long and the second is silent*

Page 100
1. C	6. A
2. B	7. B
3. A	8. A
4. B	9. B
5. B	10. C

Page 101
1. B	6. B
2. C	7. C
3. A	8. B
4. C	9. C
5. C	10. A

Page 102
1. thōse̸	6. smīle̸
2. ōpa̸l	7. māde̸
3. fŏp	8. rōa̸d
4. lăd	9. wrēa̸the̸d
5. whīle̸	10. flāke̸

Page 103
1. clēa̸n	6. stōle̸
2. nāme̸	7. knīfe̸
3. mōle̸	8. rīde̸
4. stāle̸	9. whĭt
5. wāste̸	10. whīte̸

c. *When there are two vowels together, the first vowel is long and the second is silent*

Page 104
1. B	6. A
2. B	7. B
3. A	8. A
4. A	9. A
5. B	10. B

Page 105
1. pēa̸ce̸	6. a̸frāi̸d
2. pāi̸l	7. trēa̸t
3. vīe̸	8. tōe̸
4. bōa̸t	9. glūe̸
5. shēe̸p	10. bēa̸ve̸r

Page 106
1. A	6. A
2. A	7. B
3. B	8. A
4. A	9. B
5. B	10. B

Page 107
1. Yes	6. Yes
2. Yes	7. No
3. No	8. Yes
4. No	9. Yes
5. Yes	10. Yes

C. *Syllabication*
1. *Knows rules for syllables*
a. *Each syllable must have a vowel and a single vowel can be a syllable*

Page 108
1. 2	11. 2
2. 2	12. 2
3. 3	13. 2
4. 3	14. 2
5. 3	15. 2
6. 3	16. 3
7. 3	17. 3
8. 3	18. 3
9. 2	19. 3
10. 1	20. 3

Page 109
1. 3	11. 5
2. 3	12. 2
3. 2	13. 2
4. 3	14. 2
5. 3	15. 3
6. 2	16. 2
7. 3	17. 1
8. 4	18. 3
9. 2	19. 5
10. 1	20. 3

Answer Key

Page 110
1. 2	11. 3
2. 2	12. 2
3. 2	13. 3
4. 3	14. 1
5. 2	15. 3
6. 3	16. 2
7. 2	17. 3
8. 3	18. 4
9. 3	19. 1
10. 2	20. 4

Page 111
1. 2	11. 3
2. 2	12. 2
3. 2	13. 2
4. 3	14. 2
5. 3	15. 2
6. 1	16. 4
7. 2	17. 2
8. 2	18. 2
9. 1	19. 3
10. 3 (2)	20. 2

b. The root is a syllable and is not divided

Page 112
1. A	6. A
2. B	7. A
3. A	8. B
4. B	9. B
5. A	10. B

Page 113
1. B	6. B
2. A	7. A
3. A	8. B
4. B	9. A
5. B	10. B

Page 114
1. (stand) ard	6. (staff) er
2. (hit) ter	7. un (fail) ing
3. (fish) y	8. (kill) er
4. dis (use)	9. sub (let)
5. (train) ing	10. tri (dent)

Page 115
1. (wait) ing	6. ap (prove)
2. re (solve)	7. a (round)
3. (plain) ly	8. (help) less
4. fore (head)	9. dis (close)
5. dis (arm)	10. (boast) ful

c. Blends are not divided

Page 116
1. tr, c	6. fl, b
2. sh, b	7. sm, c
3. cr, c	8. dr, a
4. gr, a	9. sl, sh, b
5. dr, c	10. pr, a

Page 117
1. sp, b	6. fr, b
2. fr, b	7. dr, b
3. fl, sh, c	8. gl, c
4. cr, a	9. pl, b
5. pr, a	10. sn, a

Page 118
1. dry ness	6. tri umph
2. flop py	7. tri ad
3. ghost like	8. spouse
4. pride ful	9. glo ry
5. sky lark	10. crowd ed

Page 119
1. creep y	6. bloat ed
2. slow ness	7. gran dee
3. drought	8. plush
4. ski er	9. try out
5. flam ing	10. chalk

d. Suffixes and prefixes are syllables

Page 120
1. in spect	6. up end
2. boy (hood)	7. seam (less)
3. act (or)	8. sub merge
4. peace (ful)	9. re duce
5. ex ile	10. whole (some)

Page 121
1. mis print	6. semi circle
2. guile less	7. re view
3. e merge	8. oil y
4. grace ful	9. do er
5. child hood	10. ex tend

Page 122
1. danc (er)	6. pre view
2. ex port	7. gut (less)
3. hu mid (ity)	8. pow er (ful)
4. in tone	9. false (hood)
5. way (ward)	10. cir cum scribe

Page 123
1. ad just	6. girl (hood)
2. jest (er)	7. hu man (ly)
3. bi sect	8. sleeve (less)
4. re vive	9. to (ward)
5. thank (ful)	10. ex haust

e. Suffix ed if preceded by a single d or t usually forms a separate syllable

Page 124
1. B	6. A
2. A	7. B
3. B	8. A
4. B	9. A
5. A	10. A

Page 125
1. A	6. B
2. A	7. A
3. B	8. B
4. B	9. A
5. A	10. B

Page 126
1. trot ted
2. stud ded
3. grant ed
4. re flect ed
5. want ed
6. knead ed
7. ex pect ed
8. con tent ed
9. deed ed
10. rest ed

Page 127
1. B
2. A
3. B
4. B
5. A
6. A
7. A
8. B
9. A
10. A

f. *If a vowel in a syllable is followed by two consonants, the syllable ends with the first consonant*

Page 128
1. C
2. B
3. A
4. A
5. B
6. C
7. B
8. B
9. C
10. C

Page 129
1. A
2. B
3. C
4. C
5. B
6. C
7. C
8. A
9. B
10. B

Page 130
1. ur gent
2. blur ring
3. pris tine
4. col lec tive
5. ac tion
6. en tire
7. cer tain
8. les son
9. par ty
10. per son

Page 131
1. b
2. d
3. a
4. b
5. c
6. c
7. b
8. a
9. c
10. c

g. *If a vowel in a syllable is followed by only one consonant, the syllable ends with the vowel*

Page 132
1. A
2. A
3. B
4. A
5. A
6. B
7. B
8. B
9. B
10. B

Page 133
1. A
2. A
3. B
4. B
5. A
6. B
7. A
8. B
9. A
10. A

Page 134
1. so da
2. sta di um
3. de lay
4. sea son
5. de fy
6. no tice
7. fo rum
8. pri vate
9. ri val
10. be fore

Page 135
1. vi tal
2. fe ver
3. mu ral
4. mu sic
5. ho ly
6. to ga
7. to ma to
8. me ter
9. ho tel
10. na val

h. *If a word ends in* le, *the consonant just before the* l *begins the last syllable*

Page 136
1. A
2. B
3. B
4. A
5. A
6. A
7. B
8. B
9. A
10. A

Page 137
1. fum ble
2. cir cle
3. la dle
4. jun gle
5. twin kle
6. stee ple
7. cra dle
8. bot tle
9. mid dle
10. muz zle

Page 138
1. cob ble
2. daw dle
3. nee dle
4. waf fle
5. gar gle
6. an gle
7. crin kle
8. rum ple
9. puz zle
10. cat tle

Page 139
1. c
2. b
3. a
4. c
5. a
6. c
7. b
8. a
9. c
10. c

i. *When there is an* r *after a vowel, the* r *goes with the vowel*

Page 140
1. co<u>rr</u>al, b
2. ba<u>r</u>becue, a
3. hu<u>rr</u>icane, b
4. o<u>r</u>ator, c
5. mo<u>r</u>bid, c
6. ma<u>rr</u>ow, a
7. transpa<u>r</u>ent, b
8. a<u>rr</u>ogant, b
9. he<u>r</u>oine, c
10. hum<u>or</u>ous, a

Page 141
1. cur tains
2. her ald
3. or bit
4. bur glar
5. re ver ber ate
6. hor ri ble
7. pro por tion
8. her ring
9. mar vels

Page 142
1. de<u>r</u>by, b
2. ga<u>r</u>den, c
3. ma<u>r</u>ket, a
4. cu<u>r</u>sive, c
5. co<u>rr</u>idor, a
6. bu<u>r</u>den, b
7. galle<u>r</u>y, a
8. co<u>r</u>sage, b
9. mode<u>r</u>ate, b
10. tole<u>r</u>ate, b

Answer Key

D. *Knows Accent Rules*
1. *In a word of two or more syllables, the first syllable is usually accented unless it is a prefix*

2. *In most two-syllable words that end in a consonant followed by y, the first syllable is accented and the last is unaccented*

3. *Beginning syllables* de, re, be, er, in, *and a are usually not accented*

4. When a suffix is added, the accent falls on or within the root word

Page 157
1. A 6. A
2. B 7. B
3. A 8. B
4. B 9. A
5. A 10. B

Page 158
1. A 6. A
2. B 7. B
3. B 8. A
4. A 9. B
5. B 10. A

Page 159
1. glam' or ous 6. port' a ble
2. Ar' a bic 7. con tent' ment
3. i' tem ize 8. sea' ward
4. com plete' ly 9. de light' ful
5. con spir' a tor 10. ad just' er

Page 160
1. his' to ry, re port', per' il ous, he ro'ics
2. pu' ri ty, re veals', ef' fort
3. bo' ny, jump' er, de cide'
4. fog' gy, re tard', de part' ing
5. re mov' al, length' ens, cus to' di an's
6. run' ner, re spect' ful
7. in' sect, re pel' lent, ef fec' tive
8. sculp' ture, hand' some, life' like, like' ness
9. a bol' ish, cov' er age, false' hoods
10. friend' ship, in cred' i ble, boun'ty, ef' fort less

Page 161
1. place' ment 6. for' ward
2. sug ges' tion 7. pro gres' sive
3. shape' less 8. dan' ger ous
4. en dur' ance 9. ner' vous ness
5. un for get' ta ble 10. pu' ri ty

5. Endings that form syllables are usually unaccented

Page 162
1. B 6. A
2. B 7. A
3. A 8. B
4. A 9. B
5. B 10. A

Page 163
1. C 6. B
2. A 7. A
3. A 8. B
4. C 9. B
5. B 10. B

Page 164
1. X 6. X
2. C 7. C
3. C 8. X
4. C 9. C
5. X 10. C

Page 165
1. board' walk 6. folk' lore
2. bro' ther hood 7. il le' gal
3. son' ny 8. bone' head
4. dom' i no 9. heav' en ward
5. sense' less ness 10. man' i fold

Page 166
1. fol' de rol 6. ton' sil
2. where' a bouts 7. tooth' less
3. kins' folk 8. men' ace
4. tail' back 9. side' line
5. wo' man hood 10. cork' screw

6. When a final syllable ends in le, *that syllable is usually not accented*

Page 167
1. A 6. B
2. B 7. B
3. A 8. A
4. B 9. B
5. A 10. A

Page 168
1. a 6. b
2. c 7. b
3. b 8. a
4. a 9. b
5. b 10. a

Page 169
1. flex' i ble 6. in' fan tile
2. hum' ble 7. pass' a ble
3. fi na' gle 8. tri' ple
4. gig' gle 9. as sem' ble
5. au' to mo bile 10. bi' cy cle

Page 170
1. i' dle 6. en tan' gle
2. hud' dle 7. wag' gle
3. di vis' i ble 8. op' er a ble
4. par' ti cle 9. glob' ule
5. gen' tle 10. ax' le

Page 171
1. peo' ple, guz' zle, whis' tle
2. bi' cy cle, sim' ple
3. han' dle, wat' tles
4. sin' gle, dou' ble, fid' dle
5. en sem' ble, fiz' zled
6. bri' dle, en cir' cle, sea' ward
7. gen' tle, mai' den, fan' ci ful, ca'per
8. strug' gle, trou' ble, scram' ble
9. stage' struck, play' er, flash' y
10. mul' ti ple, shut' tle, car' ry, pluck'y, hil' ly

Answer Key

E. Knows Possessives

Page 172
1. The president's followers
2. The football player's clowning
3. The umpire's decision
4. The bats' wings
5. Phyllis's brother and James's son
6. The teacher's patience
7. The aged leader's wisdom
8. Democracy's champions
9. Charlie's misfortunes
10. The actors' strike

Page 173
1. The fruit basket's contents were ripe and sweet.
2. The searchers' signal was awaited with anxiety.
3. My mother's new suit is a popular color this season.
4. The thermometer's mercury is down to zero.
5. Amy's book bag has the face of a clown (a clown's face) on it.
6. Nathan's ice skates are dull and need sharpening.
7. Mabel's story was fantastic and very funny.
8. Gus's homework disappeared from his desk.
9. Andrew's red sports car gets twenty-five miles per gallon.
10. The interstate highway's good safety record improved with the lower speed limit.

Page 174
1. The book's title is *Stories of Faith*.
2. Burn victims' scars fade with time.
3. San Francisco's cable cars are both a tourist attraction and a means of transportation.
4. The carpet cleaner's powerful machine cleans quickly and well.
5. The car's faulty generator caused a breakdown.
6. The checkbook's balance did not coincide with the bank statements.
7. The film's ending brought loud applause.
8. The Smiths' dog tore the mailman's trousers.
9. The marathon racer's exhaustion slowed his pace.
10. The crowd's yells upset the batter.

Page 175
1. The candidates' speeches were rip-roaring.
2. The artist's palette was a blurb of colors.
3. The ruler's ragged edge cut my thumb.
4. The village's many antique shops are filled with quaint and curious things.
5. The tour guide's comments were interesting.
6. Motorcycle riders' helmets are for safety.
7. The city library's record collection includes popular and classical music.
8. Police cars' flashing lights demand the right of way.
9. St. Louis's gateway arch recalls the history of the city as the gateway to the West.
10. School athletes' letters indicate the sport in which they participated.

Page 176
1. The seven sisters' father was ninety years old.
2. Geologists flew over the volcano's crater.
3. Mr. Short painted his child's desk.
4. Everyone went swimming in the boss's pool.
5. You cannot tell a book's contents by the book's cover (by its cover).
6. The three dogs' tails kept wagging.
7. Kevin insisted he had not heard his mother's request.
8. Jane denied seeing her sister's cat.
9. The weatherman's forecast was accurate.
10. Thrown rocks cracked the car's windshield.

F. Knows Contractions

Page 177
1. It is
2. I would
3. cannot
4. I had
5. has not
6. did not
7. They are
8. They will
9. We have
10. would not

Page 178
1. won't
2. isn't
3. don't
4. hasn't
5. hadn't
6. haven't
7. We'll
8. It'll
9. couldn't
10. She's

280

Page 179
1. He'd
2. She'll
3. I'll
4. They've
5. It's
6. We'd
7. We'd
8. I've
9. You'll
10. You've

Page 180
1. I am
2. should not
3. was not
4. We are
5. He is
6. shall not
7. does not
8. You had
9. They had
10. You have

Page 181
1. That is, we are
2. had not
3. were not
4. You would
5. You have
6. It'll
7. She'd
8. Don't
9. doesn't
10. We'll

G. *Knows Silent Letters*

Page 182
1. sight
2. wring
3. knot
4. thumb
5. gush
6. gherkin
7. knee
8. gnarl
9. bomb
10. thought
11. know
12. wreck

Page 183
1. C
2. knew
3. C
4. C
5. C
6. C
7. C
8. C
9. C
10. plumbing
11. knight
12. weird

Page 184
1. C
2. ticktock
3. C
4. C
5. wreath
6. knife
7. C
8. C
9. knapsack
10. C
11. C
12. C

Page 185
1. ghetto
2. plumb
3. pitcher
4. gnaw
5. knack
6. wrap
7. portray
8. solemn
9. straight
10. toast
11. ruler
12. numb

Page 186
1. pitch
2. gnu
3. dumb
4. kneeler
5. column
6. bough
7. lumber
8. conscience
9. plague
10. knickers
11. plumber
12. shoulder

H. *Knows Glossary*

Page 187 Words crossed out:
1. female
2. appointed
3. To win wars
4. tribune
5. four
6. Roman
7. a political party
8. Patricians
9. Aristocracy
10. plebs

Page 188
1. instrument showing how high plane is from ground
2. 76
3. de/scent, 64
4. body of plane without wings
5. hăng′ərs, buildings for aircraft storage
6. 3, pro/pel/ler
7. part that helps steer
8. 5, distance one can see or be seen
9. 99, plane with two sets of wings, one above the other

Page 189
1. 4
2. 88
3. under biology
4. sudden sliding of mass of snow, ice, rocks, etc., down mountain slope
5. brachial
6. botany
7. 4
8. 80 and 101
9. frog, toad, newt, salamander
10. botanist

Page 190
1. 72
2. 5
3. compressor
4. delirium
5. geologist
6. very cold or freezing
7. geology
8. amphibians and reptiles
9. cellular

Page 191
1. hydroelectric
2. northern lights
3. fertile
4. section of a canal
5. 99
6. topography
7. maritime
8. blocks of hard snow, igloos
9. lichen

Answer Key

COMPREHENSION

A. Outlining

1. Takes notes effectively

Page 192
A. 1. Supernatural beings
2. Special powers of magic and enchantment
B. 1. From very early times
2. In all literatures
C. 1 Tiny, wizened-faced old men
2. Beautiful enchantresses
3. Hideous, man-eating giants or ogres
D. 1. Underground
2. In the sea
3. In an enchanted forest
4. In a faraway land
E. 1. Arabic jinn
2. Scandinavian troll
3. German elf
4. English pixie

Page 193
A. 1. Flat/level
2. Treeless
B. 1. From western Ohio to the Rockies
C. 1. Rich in organic matter
2. Large quantities of nutrients
3. Excellent structure
4. Good water-holding capacity
D. 1 Pampas—Argentina
2. Llanos—northern South America
3. Steppes—Eurasia
4. High Veld—South Africa
E. 1. Wheat

Page 194
A. 1. Texas Rangers
2. Canadian Mounties
3. Desert Patrol
B. 1. Mounties: canoe, dog sled, snowmobiles
2. Desert Patrol: camels, jeeps, helicopters
C. 1. Dress
2. Area patrolled
3. Work
D. 1. Drought
2. Movement of wanderers to towns and cities
3. Camels replaced by jeeps and pickup trucks

Page 195
A. 1. Egypt
2. 2700 B.C.
B. 1. Flowers

Page 195
2. Leaves
3. Roots
4. Herbs
C. 1. Paris
2. London
3. New York
4. Moscow
D. 1. Near pyramids: jasmine, roses, cassia, lemon-grass, geraniums, basil, mint
2. North of Cairo: carnations, violets, bitter orange
E. 1. Children harvest
2. Use thumb and forefinger
3. Each blossom picked individually

2. Can sequence ideas or events

Page 196
a. 6   h. 1
b. 3   i. 8
c. 14   j. 5
d. 4   k. 13
e. 9   l. 7
f. 2   m. 12
g. 11   n. 10

Page 197
a. 7   h. 5
b. 2   i. 8
c. 10   j. 3
d. 1   k. 6
e. 4   l. 9
f. 13   m. 12
g. 11

Page 198
a. 4   h. 12
b. 10   i. 3
c. 7   j. 9
d. 1   k. 5
e. 6   l. 8
f. 2   m. 11
g. 13

Page 199
a. 9   j. 3
b. 6   k. 15
c. 12   l. 11
d. 8   m. 1
e. 5   n. 7
f. 13   o. 17
g. 4   p. 16
h. 14   q. 2
i. 10

3. Can skim for specific purposes
a. To locate facts and details

282

Page 200
1. War victims stream into towns.
2. They have clothes on their backs and few possessions.
3. First bus stop for Salisbury at Musika in Harare.
4. Many get off there having no other place to go.
5. Town squatters are there, too.
6. Live by begging, making simple articles to sell, rummaging in rubbish dumps.
7. Refugees from Mozambique cannot return to their country because the borders are closed.
8. Their status is against the law; any shelter they try to build is torn down by the authorities.
9. People with no place to stay live in the open.
10. Red Cross, churches, etc., are trying to help.

Page 201
1. U.S. has come of age, with its bicentennial.
2. Its struggle is recorded:
   a. In minds of those who lived it and told it to their children
   b. In articles they made and used
   c. In letters, accounts
   d. In restored villages
   e. In antique stores
   f. By antique collectors

Page 202
1. To provide easy and speedy access to cities; to increase speed of travel between cities.
2. Roads were needed; building them provided jobs.
3. By women pushing baby carriages so bulldozers could not move.
4. To see plans beforehand.
5. Alternatives were suggested that were efficient, not destructive. Changes were made.
6. Because of increased costs of labor and materials.
7. That of restoring and preserving old buildings.

Page 203
1. De Lesseps was an engineer and diplomat.
2. Associated with Suez and Panama Canals.
3. Life spanned nineteenth century.
4. Served in Spain and Egypt.
5. Got permission, raised money, supervised construction of Suez Canal.
6. Became president of company for Panama Canal.
7. Problems: disease, money, planning.
8. Bankruptcy: trial, sentenced.
9. Did not go to prison.
10. Rights purchased by U.S.

b.   To select and reject materials to fit a certain purpose

Page 204 A. *Things you don't have to do:*
1. get up at a certain time
2. get to school on time
3. have certain classes at set times
4. do what the teachers decide
5. pack a lunch
   B. *Things that become fun include:*
1. getting up when you feel like it
2. reading
3. the exercise you choose
4. peanut butter and jelly sandwiches

Page 205   *Use of sails on rigs resulted in:*
1. increased speed
2. decreased roll
3. decreased drag
4. decreased use of fuel
5. saving of time
6. saving of fuel
7. saving of money
   Experience with sails may be applied to:
1. other tugs
2. coastal freighters
3. ocean-going vessels

Answer Key

Factors contributing to development of Hudson Valley wineries:
1. new breed of owners
2. use of hybrid vines
3. angle of slopes
4. kind of soil
5. influence of Hudson River on climate
6. new laws
7. tax breaks

Page 207 *Self-discipline comes from:*
1. training yourself, listening to "you ought to"
2. pushing away temptations
3. hard work
4. persistence

It results in:
1. achievement
2. strength
3. productivity
4. success

Examples of self-disciplined persons:
1. baseball pitchers
2. boxers
3. musicians
4. doctors
5. artists
6. runners

4. Can identify main ideas of paragraphs

Page 208
1. Bridges get people and vehicles from one point to another across something.
2. Earliest bridges were made of logs, vines, or woven fibers.
3. Later, stones and bricks were used to build arched bridges.
4. Wood, used later, is not suitable because it rots and burns.
5. Cast iron was used next but it was too rigid.
6. The discovery of steel revolutionized bridge-building because it is a flexible material.

Page 209
1. A calendar is a system of reckoning time.
2. Records of observations of the sun and the moon are the basis for calendars.
3. Differences in the cycles of the sun and the moon cause calendar problems.
4. Intercalation is used to combine the lunar and the solar year.
5. A record of the past and plans for the future made calendars necessary.

Page 210
1. Reading is the mind interpreting symbols.
2. Before the printing press, reading was the special skill of only a few.
3. Today, reading is vital for all because everything is in print.
4. The battle against illiteracy goes on.

Page 211
1. Rock music is a combination of several black and white music styles.
2. Beatles and Dylan were responsible for the change of rock-and-roll to rock.
3. Rock-and-roll made black rhythm and blues understandable to whites.
4. Rock-and-roll is for and about adolescents.

5. Can interpret characters' feelings

Page 212 A. 1. cheerful, 2. pride, 3. angry
B. Words crossed out: regret, worry, resentment
C. anxious, worried, frightened, frantic, afraid

Page 213 A. Words crossed out: self-centered, rude, insensitive, unappreciative
B. Words crossed out: spiteful, irresponsible, reckless

Page 213 C. lost, strange, afraid, hesitant, daring, courageous, reassured

Page 214 A. 1. cheerful, eager, kind, thoughtful, courteous, humorous
2. consideration for her, kindness, concern, love, caring, patience, solicitude
B. They felt good about themselves, satisfied about what they had done, generous and happy. A good day's work gives satisfaction. They had enjoyed being together. They felt generous because they had done something for somebody other than themselves.

Page 215 A. 1. pleased, proud, happy, wanting to share yet hesitant to do so
2. worried, concerned, proud, understanding, caring
3. sincere, dedicated, hard-working, not wanting to brag
B. worry, dismay, hopelessness, disappointment, unwillingness to give up, courage, determination

6. *Can identify topic sentences*

Page 216 1. Seasoning with herbs and spices is no mystery.
2. The classic shirtdress may be worn everywhere.
3. The education of 45 million young Americans is a very important matter.
4. The essential needs of children must be met.

Page 217 1. It was a holiday.
2. Some herbs enhance the flavor of certain foods more than others.
3. Our new gift catalog contains over 200 items.
4. There had been no rain for weeks.

Page 218 1. A classic dress is suitable for wearing everywhere and forever.
2. We all begin to wish for change.
3. Eclectic means selecting and using the best elements of all systems.
4. New FCC proposals would put possibly thousands of new television stations on the air.

Page 219 1. In science, not infrequently a creative leap forward is made.
2. Where we live contributes much to what we are.
3. Zoos have changed.
4. Size is often not important in choosing a dog.

B. *Following Directions*

Page 220
to 223
Correct information in proper spaces. Directions should be followed meticulously.

C. *Drawing Conclusions*

Page 224 1. To watch a parade
2. To scenes of his youth, his boyhood home, to visit a relative
3. At the dentist's office.

Page 225 1. By train
2. Never
3. To San Francisco
4. The President

Page 226 1. A politician
2. A teacher
3. To the beach
4. Away from home or in a motel or hotel room
5. Dusk, evening

Answer Key

Page 227
1. Because he did not want her tagging along
2. a. The walk would be too much for her five-year-old sister.
   b. She was tired and frustrated.
3. Thanksgiving

D. Reading for Verification

Page 228
1. a. No. The ad says to apply in person.
2. b. Two butchers are needed. Your cousin said "a butcher."
2. Yes. They need regulars and substitutes.
3. G
4. H. No experience necessary
5. Southvale

Page 229
1. No. They want people who desire to make a career of being security officers.
2. D. Shoes
3. Large. It is a chain store.
4. B. Some lifting of ceramic tiles is part of the job.
5. E. Shipping

Page 230
1. True
2. False
3. True
4. False
5. False
6. True
7. True
8. True
9. False
10. True

Page 231
1. False
2. False
3. False
4. False
5. True
6. False
7. True
8. False
9. False
10. False

E. Locating Information
1. Reference material
a. Can read and interpret graphs

Page 232
1. 9240
2. Thursday
3. 9420
4. Wednesday
5. no
6. higher
7. average or midpoint
8. 60
9. 60
10. three

Page 233
1. 17
2. 17
3. Yes, 10
4. Third
5. Ninth
6. 2
7. 44
8. c and d
9. Same
10. a and b

Page 234
1. 824
2. between 840 and 842
3. sharp, fast, great
4. between Thursday and Friday
5. average or midpoint
6. 2
7. 3
8. Thursday
9. Monday

Page 235
1. Saturday
2. Monday
3. It levels off midweek on Wednesday and Thursday
4. Between Thursday and Friday
5. Equally low between Saturday and Sunday and between Sunday and Monday
6. No
7. Thursday
8. Yes, Sunday
9. No
10. Friday

b. Can read and interpret maps

Page 236
1. Via the Jamestown-Newport Ferry
2. southernmost
3. Broadway becomes Rte. 114
4. South on Bellevue Ave., east on Ruggles Ave.
5. Touro Synagogue
6. Bellevue Ave. and Bath Rd.
7. U.S. Naval War College
8. Goat Island
9. Fall River
10. Narragansett Bay

Page 238
1. Battery
2. bridge, tunnel
3. b, d, f, a, h, g, e, c
4. Broadway
5. Exchange, Wall
6. tunnel
7. elevated
8. United States
9. marine, boat, ship
10. City Hall

Page 240
1. Rockland, Westchester, Hudson
2. Piermont
3. 9W
4. state
5. 33, 9W, Closter Road
6. Irvington/Hastings-on-Hudson (Ardsley-on-Hudson acceptable)
7. Old Croton Trailway State Park
8. Birch Brook
9. Parkway
10. Tallman Mountain, swampy, low, or uninhabitable

Page 242
1. countries, Canada
2. Ontario, New York
3. Niagara River
4. Horseshoe Falls, Bridal Veil Falls, American Falls
5. Robinson Island
   Green Island
   Bird Island
   Goat Island
   Brother Island
   Three Sisters Islands
6. Horseshoe, Canada
7. Yes, above (or north)
8. Portage Avenue
9. Robert Moses Parkway
10. Customs

c. Can locate materials in encyclopedia

Page 244
1. 16; Longfellow, Henry W.
2. 3; Baseball
3. 28; Texas
4. 10; Galaxy
5. 6; Cologne
6. 25; Rock music
7. 13; Hunchback of Notre Dame
8. 9; Fry, Christopher
9. 28; Television
10. 19; Motion picture

Page 245
1. 19; Moon *or* 27; Space
2. 21; Oil
3. 6; Credit card
4. 4; Buddhism
5. 9; Fromm, Erich
6. 26; Schweitzer, Albert
7. 21; Operetta
8. 30; Zen
9. 23; Pointillism
10. 7; Daguerreotype

Page 246
1. 27; Steam engine
2. 29; Williamsburg
3. 2; Argentina
4. 3; Berlin, Irving
5. 29; Witches
6. 21; Oedipus
7. 21; Oceanography
8. 28; Thebes
9. 11; Guns
10. 24; Queen, Ellery

Page 247
1. 28; Tony Awards
2. 15; Khayyam, Omar
3. 2; Antiques
4. 3; Beatles
5. 2; Antony, Mark
6. 9; Furniture
7. 12; Hagiography
8. 15; Kilmer, Joyce
9. 18; Mexico
10. 23; Pyramids

d. Uses dictionary regularly

Page 248
1. sil-hou-et-ted
2. ar-du-ous
3. prim-i-tive
4. en-act
5. au-then-tic-i-ty
6. eager, greedy
7. to make larger or fuller, to add to what has been said or written
8. weighty, bulky
9. of sober character, sedate, steady
10. to recover, find again

Page 249
1. exchange, trade
2. captivate
3. charity, benevolence
4. pet idea, hobby
5. crawl, creep
6. rän'/dā/vōō: appointed place of meeting, a meeting by agreement
7. rep'/li/kə: exact copy or reproduction
8. kī/ot'e: small wolf
9. di/kath'/län: an athletic contest in ten separate events
10. fə/nä'/lē: end or close, termination of series of events, last act or closing of a scene
11. dek'/ād: a group of ten, a period of ten consecutive years
12. lab'/ə/rinth: building or structure with many confusing passages, a maze
13. gri/mās': to make faces
14. däs'/'l: easy to teach
15. rə/kō'/kō: overelaborate style of decoration, in odd or bad taste

Page 250
1. in'/tə/māt: hint, imply, make known indirectly
2. sək/sinkt': clearly expressed in very few words
3. pur'/jər: to swear falsely, to break a vow
4. ak'/rid: sharp or bitter to the tongue
5. iks/krōō'/shē/āt/ing: torturing, tormenting
6. one who legally has the care of the person or property of another, *keeper/caretaker*

Answer Key

Page 250   7. a slight brisk flight, *attack/ contest/engagement*

8. act of trying to equal or excel, *contention/contest/opposition*

9. good-natured pleasantry or teasing, *badinage/irony/derision/ railery*

10. one who practices any art, study, or sport for pleasure but not for money, *dilettante*

2. Library skills
a. Uses card catalog

Page 251
1. c	6. a
2. a	7. b
3. d	8. b
4. b	9. a and b
5. c	10. c

Page 252
1. 821 P
2. subject
3. Albert Luke
4. Card A
5. No
6. *Sorry We're Out of Gas*—Herhigh
7. *The Lever and the Pulley*
8. Card A
9. Last name of author begins with it
10. 821 P, 796 C

Page 253
1. A-Br	6. Ha-Ki
2. Kj-L	7. A-Br
3. O-P	8. W
4. M-N	9. Kj-L
5. Kj-L	10. Ha-Ki

Page 254
1. True	6. True
2. True	7. True
3. True	8. False
4. False	9. False
5. True	10. True

b. Understands book classification system

Page 255
1. 600-699	6. 100-199
2. 400-499	7. 800-899
3. 500-599	8. 900-999
4. 900-999	9. 000-099
5. 800-899	10. 600-699

Page 256
1. 600-699	6. 700-799
2. 400-499	7. 700-799
3. 700-799	8. 400-499
4. 600-699	9. 500-599
5. 600-699	10. 000-099

3. Periodical reading
a. Reads newspapers regularly
Page 257
and Page 258
Answers will vary according to newspaper and articles/editorials used.

Note: What is involved here and in skill E.3.c. ("Reads magazines regularly") is the objective of helping the pupil to acquire a habit. That requires repetition of the act until it becomes second nature. It requires time.

It is therefore recommended that these drills be used on a regular basis. It is unrealistic to give a pupil an assignment once and expect that from having done it once, a habit has been acquired.

For the newspaper skill, a drill might be used every day for a week or two, then once a week or some such regular pattern. For the magazine skill, a drill might be used once a week or every other week regularly for the entire school year. Even then, there is no guarantee; but at least an honest effort will have been made to establish a habit.

In both cases, a variety of kinds of articles to be read is recommended. Otherwise, one pupil may never read anything but the sports section, one might never read the editorials or the obituaries.

b. Knows major sections of newspapers
Page 259
1. A		8. B
2. M		9. C
3. C		10. C
4. D		11. Viewpoint
5. E		12. Where to Go? Magazi
6. 15A		13. Death notices
7. M (Young World)		14. What's Ahead
		15. opinion

Page 260
1. 30	6. 31
2. 48	7. 38
3. 4	8. 42
4. 34, 35	9. 34, 35
5. 38	10. 21

c. Reads magazines regularly

Page 261   Answers will vary according to magazines and articles chosen. See the *Note* for pages 257-258 above.

d. Uses periodicals for current information

Page 262
1. K	6. L
2. F	7. C
3. J	8. B
4. H	9. G
5. A	10. D

Page 263   Answers will vary according to magazines selected.

F. Can Read Proof Marks

Page 264   Frozen Waterways

Since we are close to the Bering Sea, our inland waterways are affected by the tide. When the great freeze-up occurs, the waterways usually have a smooth ice cover. An exception occurs when the cold wind is strong and blows the freezing water into piles of "broken glass" along the windward shoreline. Once the surface is frozen hard and the tide begins to swell in under the ice, the swelling water underneath and the pressure from the weight of the snow above cause the ice to crack open and lift up into giant ledges in spots. The swelling water comes through the cracks and creates a new foamy ice cover along the river banks which freezes from the top and leaves open pockets underneath as the tide recedes. The kids love to walk on the ice pockets and crack them open. There is plenty of solid ice beneath so there is no danger.

Page 265   The Family Room

Well planned, comfortable, and uncluttered—such should a family room be. Furniture should be arranged and balanced for easy communication and dining. A rug would add interest and create a focal point in front of the fireplace. The dining area is away from family room traffic yet keeps an easy corner of its own. The window wall has been kept uncurtained so that the view of the rolling hills is not lost.

Page 266   A Boy's Room

A boy's room in shades of sand and brown has a whole wall of cork for basketball posters and photos. Desk and chest are mostly white with natural oak. The key decorative elements are blinds in vanilla striped with sand and brown for graphic interest, taking from the sand and brown of the walls. At night, they are closed for privacy. The comforter repeats stripes and introduces blue.

Page 267   Optimistic

Optimistic enthusiasm is a malady peculiar to youth. In my short life, I have witnessed numerous tragic events but I truly believe that our society is stronger because of having to solve these problems, stronger because the problems are being faced, discussed, and solutions are often found. I am optimistic about the future because the immediate past with all its problems has been favorable to me.

Class Record of Reading Skills
SIXTH LEVEL

On the following pages you will find copies of a Class Record of Reading Skills: SIXTH LEVEL. This can be used to record the progress of your entire class or an individual child in mastering the specific skills at the Sixth Level.

The Class Record can help you identify groups of students who need instruction in a particular skill and to assess the relative strengths and levels of individual students. The Class Record can also be used in conferences with administrators, parents, and students to discuss reading skills progress.

CLASS RECORD OF

READING SKILLS

SIXTH LEVEL

Student Names

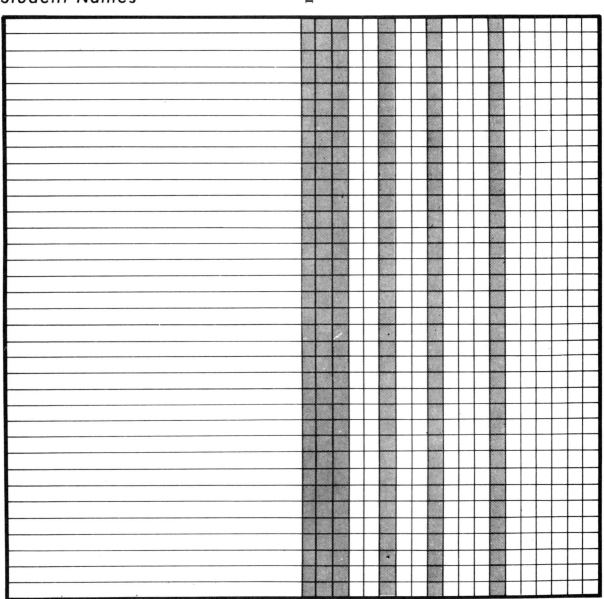

I. VOCABULARY
A. **Word recognition**
  1. Uses context clues
    a. How the word is used in sentence
    b. Function of word
  2. Uses configuration clues
    a. Visual impression of words
    b. Shape, length of words
  3. Uses language rhythms
    a. Rhyming clues
    b. Rhythm of well-expressed ideas
B. **Knows and uses prefixes and suffixes**
C. **Word meaning**
  1. Knows multiple meanings of words
  2. Can associate words and feelings
  3. Formal and informal language
    a. Identifies different speech patterns
    b. Understands level of language usage
  4. Distinguishes between aided and unaided recall

5. Can hyphenate words
6. Can provide synonyms
7. Can provide antonyms
8. Understands homophones
9. Understands homographs
10. Can write metaphors
11. Can write similes

II. WORD ATTACK SKILLS

A. Phonic and structural characteristics of words
1. Knows initial consonants and blends
2. Knows short and long vowels

B. Vowel sounds
1. Knows vowel rules
   a. One vowel in a word or syllable
   b. Two vowels in a word or syllable
   c. Two vowels together

C. Syllabication
1. Knows rules for syllables
   a. Each syllable has a vowel
   b. Root word is a syllable
   c. Blends are not divided
   d. Suffixes and prefixes are syllables
   e. Suffix -ed if preceded by single d or t
   f. Vowel followed by two consonants
   g. Vowel in syllable followed by one consonant
   h. Word ending in le
   i. R after a vowel

D. Knows accent rules
1. First syllable usually accented unless a prefix
2. Consonant followed by y
3. De, re, be, er, in and a are not accented
4. Accent falls on or within the root word
5. Endings usually unaccented
6. Final le usually not accented

E. Knows possessives
F. Knows contractions
G. Knows silent letters
H. Knows glossary

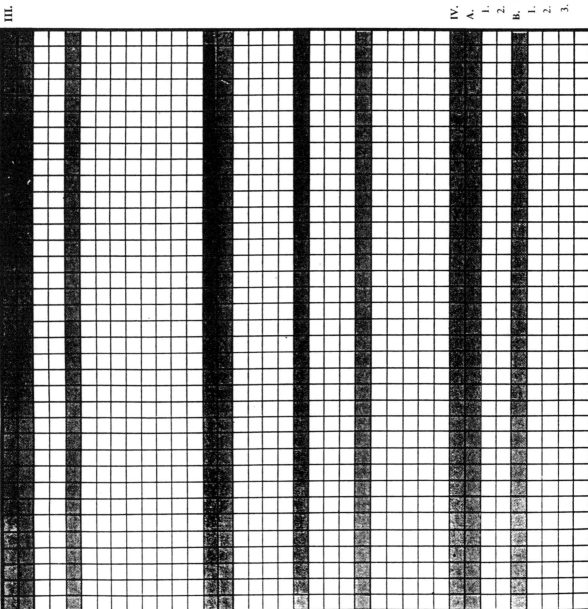

III. COMPREHENSION
  A. Outlining
    1. Takes notes effectively
    2. Can sequence ideas or events
    3. Can skim for specific purposes
      a. To locate facts and details
      b. To select and reject materials to fit a certain purpose
    4. Can identify main ideas of paragraphs
    5. Can interpret characters' feelings
    6. Can identify topic sentences
  B. Following directions
  C. Drawing conclusions
  D. Reading for verification
  E. Locating information
    1. Reference material
      a. Can read and interpret graphs
      b. Can read and interpret maps
      c. Can locate materials in encyclopedia
      d. Uses dictionary regularly
    2. Library skills
      a. Uses card catalog
      b. Understands book classification system
    3. Periodical reading
      a. Reads newspapers regularly
      b. Knows major sections of newspapers
      c. Reads magazines regularly
      d. Uses periodicals for current information
  F. Can read proof marks

IV. ORAL AND SILENT READING
  A. Oral reading
    1. Reads aloud with expression
    2. Reads with confidence and correct phrasing
  B. Silent reading
    1. Reads without lip movements
    2. Adjusts rate depending on material being read
    3. Can read 180 words per minute in fiction at grade level

Comments...

Comments...

CLASS RECORD OF

READING SKILLS

SIXTH LEVEL

Student Names

I.	VOCABULARY
A.	Word recognition
1.	Uses context clues
a.	How word is used in sentence
b.	Function of word
2.	Uses configuration clues
a.	Visual impression of words
b.	Shape, length of words
3.	Uses language rhythms
a.	Rhyming clues
b.	Rhythm of well-expressed ideas
B.	Knows and uses prefixes and suffixes
C.	Word meaning
1.	Knows multiple meaning of words
2.	Can associate words and feelings
3.	Formal and informal language
a.	Identifies different speech patterns
b.	Understands level of language usage
4.	Distinguishes between aided and unaided recall

5. Can hypenate words
6. Can provide synonyms
7. Can provide antonyms
8. Understands homophones
9. Understands homographs
10. Can write metaphors
11. Can write similes

II. WORD ATTACK SKILLS

A. Phonic and structural characteristics of words
1. Knows initial consonants and blends
2. Knows short and long vowels

B. Vowel sounds
1. Knows vowel rules
   a. One vowel in a word or syllable
   b. Two vowels in a word or syllable
   c. Two vowels together

C. Syllabication
1. Knows rules for syllables
   a. Each syllable has a vowel
   b. Root word is a syllable
   c. Blends are not divided
   d. Suffixes and prefixes are syllables
   e. Suffix ed preceded by single d or t
   f. Vowel followed by two consonants
   g. Vowel in syllable followed by one consonant
   h. Word ending in le
   i. R after a vowel

D. Knows accent rules
1. First syllable usually accented unless a prefix
2. Consonant followed by y
3. De, re, be, er, in, and a are not accented
4. Accent falls on or within the root word
5. Endings usually unaccented
6. Final le usually not accented

E. Knows possessives

F. Knows contractions

G. Knows silent letters

H. Knows glossary

III. COMPREHENSION
A. Outlining
  1. Takes notes effectively
  2. Can sequence ideas or events
  3. Can skim for specific purposes
    a. Locate facts and details
    b. Select materials
  4. Can identify main ideas of paragraphs
  5. Can interpret characters' feelings
  6. Can identify topic sentences
B. Following directions
C. Drawing conclusions
D. Reading for verification
E. Locating information
  1. Reference material
    a. Can read and interpret graphs
    b. Can read and interpret maps
    c. Can locate materials in encyclopedia
    d. Uses dictionary regularly
  2. Library skills
    a. Uses card catalog
    b. Understands book classification system
    c. Has library card
  3. Periodical reading
    a. Reads newspapers regularly
    b. Knows sections of newspapers
    c. Reads magazines regularly
    d. Uses periodicals for current information
F. Can read proof marks

IV. ORAL AND SILENT READING
A. Oral reading
  1. Reads aloud with expression
  2. Reads with confidence and correct phrasing
B. Silent reading
  1. Reads without lip movements
  2. Adjusts rate depending on material being read
  3. Can read 180 words per minute in fiction at grade level

Comments...

Comments...